BEEKEEPING

The Complete Crash Course on Raising Your Own First Backyard Bee Colonies to Achieve Self-sufficient Honey Harvest in Safe Hives

WILFRED C. BEATTY

Table of Contents

Introduction

Beekeeping is important for maintaining sustainable food production. The goal of this Beekeeping Bible is to instruct new beekeepers on how to use beekeeping concepts in their day-to-day activities. In this book, we're going to provide you with general tips on how to start beekeeping.

We have included the most beneficial methods used in contemporary beekeeping by referring to the concepts and practices found through extensive research. This book presents you with the most recent information on how to begin your bee venture. This book will assist you in starting beekeeping, whether it's as a hobby or a future business endeavor.

Chapter 1
Basics of Beekeeping

What is Beekeeping?

Beekeeping is a practice used for a variety of private and business objectives by farmers, scientists, hobbyists, and businesspeople. Bees are domesticated through this procedure in order to use their products or help pollinate crops in the field. The most well-known bee product is honey and others include beeswax, pollen, propolis (bee glue), and jelly.

The practice of beekeeping aims to closely resemble how bees live in the wild. We maintain bee colonies in artificial hives rather than allowing them to create natural combs in areas close to human properties. Bees choose to reside in wooden hives as their home. A family of bees made up of castes is called a colony. Typically, Apis mellifera honeybees are the species of bees housed in these hives.

Beekeepers raise bees on a big scale while adhering to precise procedures for repopulating the bee population for producing honey and pollination. To assist other beekeepers in establishing their own businesses, some beekeepers sell their bees and beekeeping supplies.

Since ancient times, people have been consuming honey. Beekeeping began 9,000 years ago, in North Africa, with the use of ceramic jars, and has continued to the present day.

What is its Impact on the World?

There has been a sharp reduction in the number of bees worldwide, and this trend is still ongoing. After the bees are extinct, humanity will only have four years to live, according to Albert Einstein. We wouldn't have enough plants without bees to transform energy into the nourishment that all living things require to exist.

Beekeeping is a simple and advantageous pastime to take up if you value the environment. The best place to start is with a hive or two. Five hives were all we had when we first began our own beekeeping business; today, we have an apiary. Nowadays, most of our rural farmers keep a small number of hives to sustain pollination (and, of course, for honey).

The agriculture and food production sectors depend heavily on bees. On average, 150 million flowers can be visited daily by a colony of 30,000 bees. The blossoms that don't bear fruits fit for human consumption will help protect the vegetation and act as a food source for other creatures and insects.

Sustainable agriculture and permaculture both require beekeeping. Agriculture would suffer greatly from the loss of bees. When beekeepers assist bees in thriving, they promote plant growth and food provisions for the entire world.

Who Are Your Co-Beekeepers?

There is a beekeeping community in every state. You can always go to the American Beekeeping Federation and the United States Department of Agriculture for guidance. Today's beekeepers have a variety of viewpoints on the subject. Every region is different, and the performance of the bees can change based on the local flora and environment.

Two bee inspectors are required by US law for each state, but due to a shortage of resources, not all states can meet this requirement. Before beginning your profession, we strongly advise you to get to know the local beekeepers by visiting their apiaries.

You can gain knowledge from thousands of beekeepers, and there are innumerable internet resources as well. The best teachers are those who have been doing it for a long time since experience is always the best teacher. Through experience and time, you will eventually rely less on information from others and will know instinctually what is best for your bees.

The Beginning

Historians frequently argue as to the precise beginning date of beekeeping. As with most historical events, it is difficult to identify a precise time and location. Some place the date at 9000 years ago, while others place it 10,000 years ago. Whatever the exact date, we know that beekeeping has been practiced for quite some time. Raising bees and gathering honey is an important tradition in many cultures.

Historians have discovered evidence that depicts beekeeping scenes or contains honeycomb. For instance, cave drawings of bee husbandry have been discovered in a variety of locales, including Asia, Southern Africa, Australia, and Europe. Prehistoric European pottery has also been discovered with indications of honeycomb.
Beekeeping was a vital aspect of farming culture when they were raising bees to collect honey for food or medicine. Bees have maintained their relevance in the contemporary day, contributing significantly to the development of agriculture, civilization, and cultural traditions.

An early depiction of beekeeping was found in a drawing from a cave near Valencia, Spain. This drawing is considered to date from the Mesolithic Period (the Stone Age), between 10,000 and 8,000 BC. In the image, a woman is seen harvesting honey from a beehive placed on a cliff, with bees swarming around her. This image not only shows that bee farming was being conducted at the time, but it also offers us a clear understanding of the farming techniques people were using.

The woman in the image is seen using a rope ladder to access the bee nest, which is visible on a cliff face. Of course, here is where most beehives are usually found (high in the trees or hidden in rock face cracks). This method of honey collection is still frequently used in some regions of the world despite being extremely risky due to the extreme height of these hives. This is a practice that has been observed among tribes in the Syrian desert as well as populations in Nepal and Sri Lanka. Honey is an integral element of these people's culture, and they depend heavily on gathering wild honey as a source of food and revenue.

The Origins of Organized Beekeeping

Of course, we wouldn't advise collecting honey by scaling enormous rock cliffs with a rope ladder. The creation and maintenance of beehives in a manner that mimics a natural habitat and ensures the safety and effectiveness of your honeybees are the exclusive topics of this book. We'll limit our discussion of organized beekeeping to the Ancient Egyptians and the Ancient Mayans, even though there are many known tales of societies that engaged in this form of beekeeping.

BEEKEEPING FROM THE ANCIENT EGYPTIANS

Ancient Egypt is the location where organized beekeeping was first documented. At that time, beekeepers kept colonies of a species of bee now known as the Egyptian Honeybee in hives made of twigs and reeds. In the majority of Egypt, by 1500 BCE, beekeeping had become a common practice, and honey had grown to such a high value that farmers would exchange it for money. Clay pots were used by beekeepers to gather their honey, which was then labeled according to its color and grade.

Ancient Egyptian society placed a lot of value on honey and beeswax. In addition to being a common food source, honey was employed for a wide range of spiritual and health-related purposes. Honey is still praised for its effectiveness as a temporary disinfectant for wounds, which the Ancient Egyptians made use of frequently. Additionally, honey was offered as a sacrifice to Egyptian deities, and honey jars were frequently placed in tombs for the deceased to take with them into the afterlife.

In addition to being a material used in mummification, beeswax was utilized to produce items like candles. Ra, the sun god in Egyptian mythology, was said to release tears that would transform into bees, and these bees would provide fertility by pollinating all the flowers along the Nile. Therefore, beekeeping was very important in this ancient culture, both practically and spiritually.

BEEKEEPING FROM THE ANCIENT MAYANS

A long-lived culture known as the Mayans was once believed to have extensive knowledge of beekeeping. In addition to the many other beekeeping skills they acquired, they were known to be extremely efficient with their farms, regularly splitting their current hives to enhance honey production and expand the bee numbers in each hive. Additionally, they understood the dangers of overharvesting a single hive and the value of leaving honey behind for the bees to eat during the winter.

Numerous Spanish records emphasize the Mayans' renown for beekeeping and how well-developed their apiaries were, which consisted of hundreds to thousands of native Stingless Honeybees. Although this species is indigenous to Mesoamerica, deforestation has tragically caused a more than 90% decline in population over the past two decades.

The Mayans constructed their hives out of materials like hollowed-out wood. These hives were frequently engraved in some form, often with symbols and decorations that identified the hive owner.
Each hive featured a single entrance in the center, through which the bees could enter and exit, as well as two additional holes at either end that were sealed off with stoppers made from tiny stone discs. Since then, several of these discs have been discovered, and they represent the earliest beekeeping-related objects ever discovered, dating from 300 BCE to 300 CE.

BEEKEEPING DURING THE MIDDLE AGES (EUROPEAN) AND COLONIAL PERIODS

The majority of medieval beekeeping techniques in Europe were heavily influenced by early techniques; farmers would look for huge trees that contained native wild honeybee nests. The beekeeper would create protective wood panels from different tree components after finding a nest. These panels served as a barrier between the nest and potential weather or predator damage. To make the nest more approachable and less dangerous, these guardians frequently chop off the tops of trees to keep them from growing too tall.

In northern Europe, this method of raising bees on trees gave rise to the so-called Bee Forests, many of which were held by either the Church or nobles.

This method's major drawback was that it was completely time-inefficient, despite the fact that these bee woods greatly benefited local European economies.

At the same time, beehives were being used in some areas of eastern Europe, including hollowed-out logs and jars made of woven baskets. These were mostly used in parts of Lithuania, Poland, and Germany.

These beekeeping techniques were advantageous in many ways, but primarily because the hives could be moved and kept more conveniently adjacent to populated areas, making harvesting and upkeep for the beekeepers much more convenient.

Stone hives known as "bee boles" were being fashioned into beehives in Britain, France, and other regions of western Europe. To shield the hives from inclement weather, they were frequently placed on south- or southeast-facing walls, close to orchards and gardens.

One of the first animals to be sent with early settlers was a European honeybee, according to ship cargo records from the colonial era, not long after America was "discovered." The ability of bees to produce beeswax, honey, and pollinate crops led to their status as valuable cargo at the time. Honey was frequently accepted during this period in place of sugar as a form of payment (which was highly taxed by the English). As a result, they served as both a valuable commodity—honey and beeswax—and a major source of income for many. Several goods, including candles, lipstick, shoe polish, and mead, were made primarily from honey and beeswax. Honeybee populations have spread widely over North America as a result of bee imports.

BEEKEEPING IN MODERN TIMES

Even though some societies continue to engage in wild beekeeping, today, organized bee farms provide the vast majority of the world's honey. The Langstroth hive is currently the most popular type of beehive setup. It consists of wooden boxes containing wooden frames that can easily be removed one at a time to gather honey and wax and to evaluate the hive's health. This hive structure is regarded as the best option for commercial or large-scale beekeeping because it is portable as well. Modern beekeepers frequently move hives to put the bees closer to the greatest feeding locations and near flowers with the maximum nectar production, depending on the season.

In Europe, later in the growing season, beekeepers routinely relocate their hives into the countryside. This is the peak heather season in the UK and the lavender flowering season in France. Migrating the hives may be troublesome, but it is worth it in the end because honey produced in hives close to these flowers is extremely exceptional and highly valued.

The most lucrative method of beekeeping in the US is, without a doubt, moving beehives. Huge fruit, nut, and berry farms get hives in tens of thousands throughout the primary growing season when they are driven on highways by enormous trucks. In order to increase crop yields, beekeepers frequently use their hives to pollinate crops like berries, alfalfa, almonds, and oranges.

Because of the enormous scale of these farms, it is not sufficient to rely just on indigenous honeybees to pollinate these crops; thus, bees are imported to assist. Overall, these activities are quite profitable, but there is debate about how the technique may endanger the health and welfare of honeybees and other pollinating species.

Supporting local beekeepers and organic agriculture as much as possible can help mitigate any hazards that wildlife may encounter in these situations.

Chapter 3
Why Do Beekeeping?

After discussing the lengthy history of beekeeping, let's review all the benefits of actually doing it yourself. We'll examine the many advantages of beekeeping in this section, along with some of the motivations behind this way of life. If you're still unsure about taking up this pastime or are looking for additional justification, this chapter is for you.

Benefits of Beekeeping

Beekeeping has a wealth of benefits for your yard as well as your general health. If you look into a handful of these, you might discover some information that you were previously unaware of.

1. It's interesting
2. It's not as expensive as you may think
3. It's beneficial to the environment
4. Benefits of honey in abundance
5. It's amazingly therapeutic
6. Great for kids
7. It benefits the regional economy
8. Bees can be placed anywhere
9. You can better establish ties to your neighborhood
10. You won't merely get honey
11. Perhaps you can get a tax break

Let's discuss each of these benefits in further detail.

IT'S INTERESTING

Bee aficionados unquestionably think that learning about beekeeping is interesting! This is most likely due to the fact that bees are much more complex than most people realize. Bees create societies with intricate roles, customs, and structures that are incredibly fascinating to study and observe. Even bees' communication techniques are fascinating. Like most things, it's also much more effective to learn something by experiencing it firsthand than it is to merely read about it in a book or on a website.

Keeping bees will also give you a newfound appreciation for the environment because of how crucially important bees are to our ecosystems as a whole. Every tree or flower you may see has probably been pollinated by bees, and learning about beekeeping will highlight how important this is.

Although most people don't think about nature in this context, active beekeepers are always thinking about them. Interesting, no?

IT'S NOT AS EXPENSIVE AS YOU MAY ANTICIPATE.

It's normal to worry about the cost while determining whether to begin a hobby like this. Any time-consuming activity that necessitates a lot of equipment must be expensive.
Or so you thought.
Beekeeping is not very expensive because it is a hobby that can support itself. Remember that beekeeping involves creating products in addition to having fun. These goods are easily marketable with the right connections and

Bees have a big impact on the environment. Giving bees a home that is secure and successful will help them prosper and survive! Even if earning money is your primary motivation for keeping bees, you can rest easy knowing that you're also doing your part to better the world while earning a decent living.

BENEFITS OF HONEY IN ABUNDANCE

networking. The money you spend on creating that new hive can therefore be thought of as an investment because you will eventually get something back from it.

The cost of the essential tools you'll need to establish a bee colony, including clothing, bees, hives, and other items, will probably be in the neighborhood of $500. This is still a bit pricey, but it is not bad compared to other hobbies like golf, scuba diving, and mountain climbing which require expensive equipment, individual instruction, a membership, or accreditation. Everything adds up! Beekeeping is, therefore, far less expensive than the alternatives and a fantastic method to make money.

Additionally, starting a beehive is unquestionably one of the more affordable solutions if you're considering collecting bees to get a taste of livestock raising. The cost of feeding, caring for, and providing the necessary area for livestock like pigs or cows is significantly higher. Therefore, beekeeping is a fantastic choice for newbies.

IT'S BENEFICIAL TO THE ENVIRONMENT

Nowadays, everyone is interested in learning how they can protect the environment. But unfortunately, there are very few ways that humans can genuinely have a significant impact beyond recycling and using less water.

However, keeping bees is a fantastic way to have a beneficial environmental influence. Bees move pollen from one plant to another, fertilizing and promoting the growth of both. Experts believe that bees produce about 30% of the food consumed worldwide. Bees and other pollinators are essential to the survival of 90% of wild plants.

Honey is known to have certain miraculous properties. It has numerous antibacterial and therapeutic effects and has been regarded for generations as liquid gold. It's a fantastic source of antioxidants, which helps reduce inflammation and ease stomach problems.

Some people assert that consuming modest amounts of honey each day can prevent allergies. A tablespoon of honey, added to a steaming cup of ginger tea, is said to work wonders in relieving a sore throat.

It has also been used for centuries as a therapy for wounds because of its inherent antibacterial and antimicrobial characteristics. Others assert that when drunk regularly, it helps improve memory.

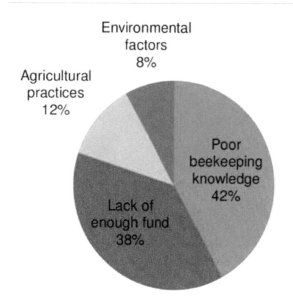

Environmental
factors
8%

Agricultural
practices
12%

Poor
beekeeping
knowledge
42%

Lack of
enough fund
38%

Honey's hydrating qualities make it a popular ingredient in skincare and haircare products as well. Some people apply it directly to their hair as a scalp treatment for conditions like dandruff, and it's a common ingredient in plenty of homemade face mask recipes.

In addition to everything said above, eating honey is generally healthy. A natural sweetener with a delightful flavor, honey is considerably healthier than processed sugar. Additionally, it is rich in vitamins and minerals like niacin, riboflavin, manganese, and iron. When honey is purchased from a grocery store, it has most likely been pasteurized, which involves boiling the honey and removing many of the aforementioned natural components. Any beekeeper will tell you that pure ingredients are the best when it comes to the flavor of honey. Even the first batch of honey you make will be superior to anything you can buy at the store.

You may come across honey branded as "wildflower honey" or "lavender honey" since the type of flower from which the bees collect their pollen also affects the flavor of your honey. If you locate your beehives close to a particular kind of bloom, you'll produce honey with a flavor that may be exceptional and unique. It's a fantastic opportunity to try new things.

IT'S AMAZINGLY THERAPEUTIC

After a hard time at work, is there anything more relaxing than spending some time in your garden? Caring for your beehive lets you experience the same sense of calm as you would taking a stroll through a lovely meadow. Beekeeping will not only keep you relaxed and quiet, but it's also a

terrific method to motivate yourself by gaining a sense of accomplishment as, like gardening, it gives you the satisfying feeling that you're contributing to something positive.

The notion that beekeeping may be calming may come as a bit of a surprise to someone who is unfamiliar with the hobby; after all, it entails interacting with hundreds of insects who could sting you if you make the wrong move. However, if you've ever engaged in beekeeping, you'll be aware that all it requires is the proper tools and techniques for it to become a leisurely activity.

GREAT FOR KIDS

It's obviously not a good idea to just toss your kids at your beehives and hope for the best. You must always keep an eye on any child who is anywhere near your beehives. Beekeeping, however, can be a really gratifying hobby for people of all ages; thus, participation should not come with an age restriction.

Kids can learn about the natural life cycles in their local environment by becoming involved in beekeeping, which is a terrific activity to introduce them to. It's also wonderful for showing kids how to cherish and enjoy nature more and how we can protect it (and why we should!).

Why not invite children from your immediate or extended family to participate in an activity day? You can demonstrate to kids all the fun and excitement beekeeping entails. You could even get in touch with nearby schools, garden clubs, or youth organizations. This is a fantastic way to use your

interest to support the neighborhood as well.

IT BENEFITS THE REGIONAL ECONOMY

It is estimated that each year, bees pollinate crops worth an astounding 15 billion dollars in America alone. Bees are responsible for the abundant agricultural yields of all types of crops farmed in the US, from cucumbers to apples. Additionally, the US honey industry is thought to be worth about $150 million.

Therefore, it follows logically that fewer bees will result in fewer crops. Higher production expenses brought on by fewer crops will eventually translate into higher product prices. Therefore, having more bees will contribute to slightly cheaper grocery store pricing for the average individual. After all, every little bit helps.

BEES CAN BE PLACED ANYWHERE

A person may be reluctant to start beekeeping for a variety of reasons, including worries about safety, finances, or time, in addition to other factors. One of the main reasons for your hesitation may be a lack of available space. After all, it must be necessary for a beehive to have a lot of open areas, and it should be as far away from structures as feasible. Right? Wrong.

First off, if placed close to a building, bees are quite unlikely to bother you because they are incredibly silent inside their hive. They can fit without producing any problems next to a farmhouse, against a wall, or even on the roof of a structure. Beehives are not as large as you might expect in terms of space. The dimensions of a typical beehive are about 20 by 16 inches, fitting inside a few square feet. If you only have one or two, you can fit them on any available plot of land.

Possessing a beehive is a hobby that doesn't have to take up much of your time. Since bees are independent beings, they don't generally need much care. With roughly 30 minutes of weekly upkeep from you and a little extra time per year to obtain your honey, bees will happily continue to work. Therefore, it wouldn't be a problem if you're putting off starting a beekeeping business because you have a full-time job and little free time.

YOU CAN BETTER ESTABLISH TIES TO YOUR NEIGH-BORHOOD

There is a good chance that you are within driving distance of a local beekeeping organization, which usually hosts occasional activities and meetings. Joining groups like these is a wonderful opportunity to meet new people, learn more about the subject, and share your enthusiasm with others in your neighborhood.

Why not approach a complete stranger at a party and ask them if they know anyone else who is interested in beekeeping? People who are new to beekeeping are frequently amazed by how many people around them are engaged in the activity.

YOU WON'T MERELY GET HONEY

We've talked about a lot of advantages of beekeeping so far, but the main one is definitely the honey you can sell or use for personal use. But there are other benefits to beekeeping besides honey.

Beehives may produce a wide variety of amazing products, such as beeswax, pollen, propolis, honeycomb, and royal jelly.

Some of these might be familiar, while others are utterly foreign. Some are foods, others are frequently found in items like candles or cosmetics, and the majority have outstanding medical advantages.

For instance, royal jelly is a substance with several health advantages, such as anti-aging and wound healing capabilities. It is frequently a component of anti-aging skincare products.

Propolis is a fantastic component that is also used for treating a wide range of skin and digestive problems as well as allergies in humans.

Your beehive will therefore generate a wide range of items, many of which are touted as superfoods in some way. It will take a bit more time and effort, but it will be well worth it to learn how to harvest each of these items. In this book, we'll only briefly discuss the harvesting of honey and beeswax.

PERHAPS YOU CAN GET A TAX BREAK

One of the key motivations for starting a beekeeping business is to make money. No matter how big or small, if your beehives generate revenue, they qualify as a business. Even if you just look after your bees occasionally and make a small profit from the honey you sell, this still counts as income, making all of the business-related equipment you purchase deductible on your yearly tax returns.

Knowing that you may deduct the modest number of tools you'll need to get started may give you a bit more peace of mind.

Make sure to schedule a meeting with an accountant or tax counselor to discuss your specific tax position if you have any questions about it.

The Business End of a Bee: The Challenges of Beekeeping

Although I absolutely enjoy keeping bees, and I hope you do as well, the reality is that it's not all fun and games. I don't want to dispel your fantasy of being covered in honey and standing in a field of wildflowers, but sometimes mistakes are made. If I didn't mention the drawbacks of beekeeping, neither you nor your bees would benefit.

If you're anything like me, you may be reading this and shaking your head while saying to yourself, "That will never happen to me." Reconsider your position. Your turn will come. You may eventually encounter difficulties comparable to those other beekeepers and I encountered, even if they are not exactly the same.

BEE STINGS

Be aware that bees sting. There's a good risk you'll get stung if you choose to keep bees. There's a good possibility you'll get stung if your neighbor decides to start keeping bees.

I find this to be the most intimidating aspect of beekeeping. Why? Due to my allergy to bee stings. Unbelievable, right? (I have never encountered a beekeeper who wasn't a little weird, including myself.) So why in the world would someone who is allergic to bees want to raise bees? Well, I like to eat, and I need bees if I want a fruitful garden. The second reason is that I now know bees don't want to sting you. I'll go into more detail regarding bee stings and how to treat them below, but you should be aware that every beekeeper I know has been stung at least once.

BEEKEEPING TAKES MUSCLE

You can harvest as much honey as 60 pounds per season. Add the weight of the hive and the bees to that, and you're going to need muscle to move the bees and their hives around. Furthermore, the hive might not always be in the ideal position for deadlifting. I firmly advise you to connect with other beekeepers in your region or enlist the assistance of a family member or friend to aid with the physical rigors of beekeeping.

BEES AREN'T FREE

You may think that bees live freely, but this is not the case. Bees can indeed be free if you are able to capture a wild swarm, build them a hive from resources you already own or receive beekeeping equipment from a trusted friend. However, this scenario is as common as a unicorn, and beekeeping will likely need a hefty upfront cost. I believe it is only fair to inform you of the beekeeping expenses so you may plan your finances.

Our start-up cost for two hives, with bees but without the apparatus for extracting honey, was roughly $1,000. Of course, this cost can vary greatly depending on the type of hive you choose to purchase, what equipment you choose to use, etc.

FINDING A BEE BABYSITTER

Something I didn't consider beforehand was that if I kept livestock, I couldn't just pick up and leave whenever I felt like it. I regret to say that I frequently encounter this issue. The good news is that, unlike many other livestock species, bees don't keep you confined to your home. But (yeah, there's always a "but") unless you have someone checking on your bees for you, you can't just pack your bags and go on a three-month vacation to the Bahamas and expect to return home to a thriving hive.

Although not impossible, it's a little more difficult to find a babysitter for bees than it is for your kid. So you might want to think again about beekeeping if you travel frequently and don't have a friend who is willing to wear a bee suit. Beekeepers protect themselves from being stung by wearing bee suits.

BAD THINGS HAPPEN TO GOOD BEES

The saddest news of all is that excellent bees still experience bad things. Your beekeeping ambitions could be dashed by the weather, nature, your neighbors, illness, poison, and other unidentified threats. Trust me; it's incredibly discouraging; I've been there and done that. Even if you follow all reasonable safety precautions, you could still lose your bees. Though it doesn't usually happen, it is possible. Just be ready to deal with this reality and keep trying. That mindset characterizes a true beekeeper.

Is Beekeeping Legal?

Does this question strike you as odd? How in the world could bees be prohibited? For God's sake, they are the foundation of nature, and without them, we would probably go hungry. The fact is that beekeeping is governed by laws in many locations across the country and even the world, particularly in communities with Homeowners Associations (HOAs). Even now, some people consider keeping bees unlawful.

Now, if this is true in your region, you could be shaking your head and preparing to dig in your heels, but I beg you: Do not get bees if they are prohibited by the law (or the rules). Instead, I advise getting involved in your county, city, or HOA board as a bee advocate; change the laws before purchasing your bee suit.

HOW TO FIND OUT IF BEEKEEPING IS LEGAL WHERE YOU LIVE

Request a copy of the bylaws, rules, or restrictive covenants if you reside in a community with an HOA, an apartment building, or a condominium complex. Check if beekeeping is covered by these laws and regulations by going through them with a fine-tooth comb. City and county regulations may not always prevail over HOA and community bylaws.

You still need to research the laws in the city or county where you live in addition to your neighborhood's rules and regulations. You should be able to get assistance from your county extension office or your city's or county's building and zoning department, all of which you can contact.

Additionally, you can get in touch with your regional land grant university or cooperative extension office, who should be able to inform you of all the regulations governing beekeeping in your county. Check online to check if your area has a local beekeepers association if you don't have a local extension office.

Chapter 4
What Do You Need To Get Started?

Bee Source

There are several ways to get bees. Among them, here are the following three best bee sources:

Established hives: The best hives are established hives, often known as second hives because they have previously been configured by an expert beekeeper. The hive he or she has been building for years is technically the one you are purchasing. It will be easier for you to get to know your bees if you add another hive around summer, if you get it early in spring, or late in the winter, and if the colony is doing a great job of reproducing. This is a great option since it enables you

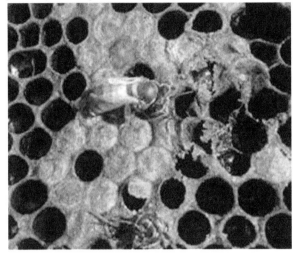

to learn about the hive and put the concepts and methods you have learned from this guide into practice.

It already has the pollen and honey that the bees and brood (eggs and young bees) need to establish themselves. However, of the three, this is the most expensive choice. Without extra materials, it costs between $350 and $400.

Package bees: A less expensive alternative is package bees, as seen on the left. It is a sizable box that contains a caged queen, bee workers, and fake sugar-based food. This is the only way you can order them online because of the secure packaging.

Bees typically cost between $95 and $135 for two pounds and between $130 and $160 for three pounds. They are simple to dump into your hive.

Since the colony will have to adjust to its new habitat and build its comb from scratch, we do not advise beginner beekeepers to use this bee source. Worker bees may reject the queen bee if the setup is improper because of the stress of the transport and the new surroundings. Additionally, during shipping, the sperm quality that has been placed in the queen suffers greatly.

The hive must accept the queen, or else it will not be able to live.

Some beekeepers wrap a food plug around the queen. If they choose to recognize her as their queen, the employees will meet their queen by consuming the meal plug and then making their way inside. When you are simply replacing worker bees in an established and well-maintained hive, package bees are advised. However, there are instances where the hive rejects newly inserted workers. After years of practice, package bees can assist you in expanding your apiary location.

Nuc colonies: The third and most popular method of getting bees is through nucleus hives (nuc hives). A smaller, transient beehive is known as a nuc. It costs $150 to $300 per nuc colony, depending on the state it is from, which is a little more than the last choice. Bees from nuc hives are all closely related, with the laying queen producing the young.

The main drawback is that the bugs and diseases that the vendor brought with them will probably come along as well. Queen rejection is not a possibility, though.

Because of this, you should exercise caution when ordering any form of the colony. Colonies are rarely shipped by shipping companies. This makes it easier to organize a meeting with the bee provider so that you can see the condition of their hives yourself. If you are unable to visit the bee providers, it is an option to seek help from your friends or the local government agency.

As supplies are limited, it is recommended to place a pre-order for bees before January or February. This enables the beekeepers to fortify your future colony in advance of its adaptation to the new environment.

This manual is based on the idea that you want to domesticate Western/European honeybees (Apis mellifera). This decision is obvious given that only Apis mellifera bees can make honey, even if you desire to keep other bee species. The Italian honeybee is a subspecies of the Western/European honeybee; its full scientific name is Apis mellifera ligustica. This may cause some confusion. Although they are largely equivalent, most beekeepers today choose the Italian bee. Carniolan, Caucasian, and Russian honeybees are other subspecies that are frequently raised in the US.

Proper Location

We shall cover the laws and guidelines for beginning your beekeeping business later in this chapter. Let's talk about where to place your apiary or honey bee hives in the meantime.

Your beehive sites' placement is crucial. Foraging possibilities, nectar and pollen sources, water, sunlight,

wind, and safety from pesticides, animals, natural disasters, and diseases should all be considered before introducing new colonies. You might also want to consider the risk of irate neighbors, as well as automobile accessibility.

The majority of hobbyist beekeepers live in suburban and residential regions. If this is you, make sure not to disturb your neighbors when working with bees. In the event that they have allergies, kindly let them know what you plan on doing.

When honeybees are introduced to a new location, worker bees will start searching the area for nectar and pollen right away. A food source ought to be found five to ten miles away. One advantage of purchasing existing or nuc colonies is that the bees already have a source of food in the hive in case they have to travel a great distance to the new location.

Set up a pan of water with stones for the bees to settle on if there isn't a natural body of water nearby. Water is essential for rearing the brood and assists in controlling the hive's temperature during the sweltering summer months.

It is crucial to have a sunny, wide area so that light may enter and the nurse bees can easily view the eggs. Bees' flight patterns are impacted by shade, which also controls the humidity in the area. There must be wind shelter provided by natural obstacles like hills, evergreen trees, structures, or other trees.

Pesticides have a harmful impact on bees' physiological processes. Because the acceptance of your business permit (organic company) will depend on the pollen the bees collect, if you intend to undertake beekeeping as a business and register as organic, make sure the farms around employ

natural farming methods. A significant no-no is using pesticides from surrounding farms.

Animals like pets, bears, reptiles, and rodents are constantly a threat. Bears can scent your hive and raid it when you least expect it, particularly in the far North.

Rodents and extreme weather, such as floods and storms, can be avoided by raising hives above the ground using cement blocks or wooden platforms. If beehives are on shoddy bases, strong gusts may cause them to tumble.

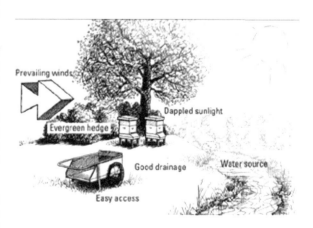

Beekeeping Equipment

This is one of the most crucial sections of this guidebook. We strongly advise you to learn more about the functions and uses of every piece of beekeeping equipment you'll need. The hive and its parts, a protective suit, a smoker, and hive tools make up the bulk of the apparatus.

A HIVE

Of course, a real beehive that your tiny companions can call home is one of the most important pieces of gear for housing a bee colony. Later on, we'll cover beehives in more detail, and chapter 9 will provide a step-by-step tutorial on how to construct your very own top-bar hive.

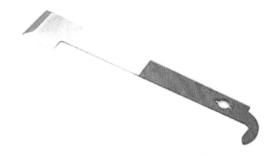

In case you weren't aware, hives are a little more intricate than just a wooden box that houses bees; in order to enhance the effectiveness of the bees' product collecting, they are designed with a variety of elements and layers.

The actual hive consists of the "nest" area inside, honey supers (where excess honey is made, kept, and retrieved by you), an exterior cover to shield it from the elements, and hive stands to keep the bottom of the hive warm and dry.

A HIVE TOOL

In essence, hive tools are just metal sticks. They can be flat or made of metal and can have a bend at the end, but they

all have the same function. This small stick comes in quite handy for many things, but its major use is for prying the hive open. You'll discover that inside your beehive, the bees use propolis, which is essentially a resin-like glue, to hold everything together. The hive tool enables you to access the hive, remove frames, scrape propolis from various locations, and more. It is quite helpful.

GLOVES

For various reasons, safeguarding your hands is equally as crucial as protecting your face. Bees can sense tense behavior through breathing, but they can also detect tenseness through trembling hands, which is the main reason novices should keep their hands covered. Many more seasoned beekeepers opt not to wear gloves because it is, of course, much simpler to maneuver around a beehive without them.

For beekeeping gloves, supple leather or other strong yet flexible materials are typically used. The material needs to be durable enough to protect you from stings while also being flexible enough to be useful. To make sure your hands and wrists are completely protected, they also frequently reach rather high up the arm (to just below the elbow). When you are looking for gloves, it's a good idea to look for ones with ventilation around the wrists because this feature will

come in handy if you're taking care of your bees on a hot day.

SMOKER

When working with bees, a smoker should always be at the ready. Before you open your hive and start digging, it can assist in quieting the bees down and overall make them more docile. In essence, this works by tricking the bees into thinking there is a potential fire threat nearby. Once they have eaten enough honey, they become considerably calmer and less likely to bite you.

The "guard bees" respond to threats to the beehive of any type by releasing a pheromone that serves as a warning to the rest of the colony. This pheromone has a banana-like smell, and if you detect it, it's definitely a good idea to emit additional smoke to cover it up. Additionally, it's generally not advised for beekeepers to consume bananas just before caring for their hive because the bees may confuse the smell for danger signals.

PROTECTIVE CLOTHING (WITH A HAT & VEIL)

There are people today who tend to their beehives without any kind of safety equipment. While more seasoned individuals may find this more comfortable, wearing safety gear is not at all shameful. Additionally, it is strongly advised to wear it if you are a newbie.

It should be stressed that the protective gear you choose should include some sort of facial protection, as bees frequently attack faces when they feel threatened. Because they are able to detect the production of carbon dioxide, bees often react violently when mammals breathe heavily (as they might do if nervous or tired). Contrary to popular belief, bees cannot sense fear, but they may detect fear-related behaviors like rapid breathing.

Therefore, it is better to keep your face entirely covered and shielded if you don't feel completely at ease with your bees. Even if you decide against investing in a full-body astronaut-style suit, at the very least shield your hands, face, and head.

BEE BRUSH

When you need to carefully transfer your bees from one comb to another, a bee brush is a helpful tool. This is required in a variety of circumstances, including when you need to collect your honey, get rid of swarms, fix broken honeycomb, etc. It's a good idea to only use the brush when absolutely necessary because your bees will despise it.

UNCAPPING KNIFE/FORK/SCRATCHER

You will require this tool when collecting honey. Wax that accumulates on top of honey cells must be removed in order to extract the honey. This process is known as "uncapping." You can easily gather honey with a single swipe of an uncapping instrument.

FEEDERS

A feeder is a tool that stores sugar syrup to provide bees with food all year round. These are useful when bees need energy and honey is inaccessible for whatever reason. Some feeders are made to go inside the hive cavity, while others are made to go at the hive entrance. An alternative is to fill a plastic food bag with sugar syrup and slice the top of the bag with a razor knife to create a makeshift feeder (about 5" long).

BUYING YOUR BEES

Therefore, the crucial question is where and how to purchase bees. Sadly, it is not as simple as going to your local grocery shop and purchasing them. You have a variety of alternatives when purchasing bees. However, you must first choose how many bees you want to purchase and how they will arrive. Additionally, FREE bees are always available, but, I'll get to that later.

There are three ways to purchase bees from bee breeders or businesses. They come in packs, nucs, and complete hives (also referred to as established colonies). My husband and I purchased packs, nucs, and feral swarm bees. Due to the

scarcity of full hives where I live, I was never able to find one when I wanted to buy one.

Each beehive you own will only require one pack or nuc to be purchased. As long as the hive doesn't expand and you don't need to add more dwelling space for the bees, a full hive will be enough.

PACKS

A pack of bees typically weighs three pounds and contains workers, drones, and a mated queen bee, which means that some drones have already visited and that she is, in a sense, pregnant. It will take some time for them to learn to know and accept the queen because she is usually not the colony's queen. The majority of the time, packs include about 10,000 bees and range in price from $50 to $80. (The basic guideline is 3,000 to 4,000 bees per pound.)

With no comb or brood, packs offer excellent value but take longer to establish. However, a lot of novice beekeepers take pleasure in watching a colony grow from nothing, so to speak.

NUCS

Nucs are drawn frames that have been set already and contain wax, honey, pollen, brood, and bees. A queen bee, workers, and drones are all found in nucs. Five frames make up the typical nuc. Nucs are an excellent investment because they are set up and prepared to begin producing as soon as you receive them.

You must buy packs if you choose a top bar or Warre hive because nucs are only utilized in Langstroth hives.

ESTABLISHED COLONY

Established colonies are more difficult to locate and slightly more expensive, but they are still a great alternative to get you started right away. They are made up of an entire hive body, which consists of 8 to 10 drawn, established frames filled with wax, pollen, honey, and bees. They bring workers, drones, and the colony's queen bee along with them. It's easiest for beginner beekeepers to start with established colonies.

Some drawbacks to established colonies are that they are expensive (almost three times higher than that of a nuc), lack availability, and are difficult to transport. If you want to make sure the colony is healthy, you should inspect it. To ensure that you are obtaining healthy bees, you should acquire a second opinion from an experienced beekeeper who can assist you with the inspection of an established colony.

Any trustworthy beekeeper or breeder will include a health guarantee with the purchase, but not all of them are. If you are getting bees from a firm or business, find out if they have a health guarantee and what to do if your bees arrive unwell or unhealthy.

FREE-BEES

Is there still such a thing as free? If you don't charge for your time, the answer to that question is yes. You may get bees for nothing in a few different methods. Since most of my recommendations require some prior beekeeping knowledge, I don't typically advocate these concepts to brand-new beekeepers.

What to Look for in Your Bees

Now that you are aware of the various methods for obtaining bees, we should talk about the qualities you should search for.

The first step is choosing the type of bees you want to keep. Yes, there are several types of bees available; the "honeybee" is not the only kind. The most common breeds are the Carniolan, Italian, Caucasian, Buckfast, and Russian varieties, and each has both positive and negative traits.

Do not worry too much about the breed, though, as all honeybee breeds are capable of interbreeding. To assist in the production of stronger genetics, most bee packages include a blend of many breeds.

Three factors should be taken into consideration while choosing bees: temperament, productivity, and adaptability to your climate.

Italian bees may thrive in a wide range of habitats, although they struggle in hot climates. They are a popular bee for beginning apiarists due to their moderate temperament, lack of propensity to swarm, and ability to produce white caps on honeycomb. Due to their large colony sizes, they are vulnerable to famine in the winter; therefore, if you live in a location with lengthy winters, you will need to make sure you supplement their nutrition significantly.

Compared to Italian bees, Carniolan bees are darker in color and originate from Yugoslavia. Carni bees are a fantastic choice to introduce to more aggressive bees because they are peaceful, kind, and simple to handle, even though they are inclined to swarm. They enjoy cool, moist settings and are more likely to go in quest of food on days that have been lightly rained.

A Carni bee colony will expand quickly if your hive has access to a lot of natural nectar, yet they are skilled at self-regulating their population. This means that a hive will grow larger if there is plenty of food. Due to the reduced colony size throughout the winter, malnutrition becomes less of an issue.

Caucasian bees are better adapted to cooler climates because they originated close to the Caspian Sea. They can more easily obtain nectar from deeper flowers thanks to their larger tongues. Their main benefit is their serenity; many beekeepers regard them as the most gentle of all honeybees. Their drawback is that they produce a lot of propolis, a sticky material that resembles glue inside the hive, making examinations more time- and labor-intensive. Finding some will be quite challenging because they are a very uncommon breed of bee.

Specialty bees like the Russian and Buckfast bee are developed from other varieties. Due to the aggressive behavior of the progeny of a naturally existing queen, Buckfast bees are not as popular as they previously were. This characteristic was so unfavorable that it eclipsed their capacity to make a lot of honey. As a result, it is quite difficult to find Buckfasts for sale in contemporary beekeeping circles.

The Russian honeybee is adapted to cold regions and has a modicum of disease resistance, but no bee breed is really immune to mites and pests. Similar to the Carniolan bee, they have fewer members in the colony during the winter but take a little longer to increase in number in the spring. However, once they do, be careful! You must keep a close eye on them because of how quickly their number can increase and how likely they are to swarm.

Keep in mind that these are merely general recommendations. The bees you purchase will typically be a mixture of various breeds, which is a positive thing! Just consider all the issues a purebred animal of any type faces; genetic diversity is advantageous since it makes your bees more robust, productive, and hardy.

Regardless of what breed you believe to be the greatest, we have a few suggestions for how to pick a breed. First, find out from neighborhood beekeepers what species of bees they raise. You might discover that the majority exclusively work with one certain breed, which suggests that those bees are optimal for your region's climate. Consider purchasing your bees from the neighborhood beekeepers if they are willing to do so, as you will know, as we have mentioned, that your bees will thrive there.

Second, place your order early in the year, wherever you buy your bees from. The longer you wait, the fewer options you will have. Preordering will ensure that your order is arranged and that you do not miss out on receiving your bees because many bee companies are extremely busy in the spring.

Depending on the space you have available for bees, you might want to think about erecting many hives. You can better monitor your bees if you have multiple hives because you'll have something to compare their activity and health to. You may even borrow from the other hive to help one hive get back on track if it starts to struggle. If you don't have enough time, space, or money for more than one hive, ask your mentor if they'd be prepared to let you borrow one of theirs to supplement yours when you need it.

RULES/REGULATIONS

The strategy used for beekeeping laws varies by region, state, country, etc. As a beekeeper, it is your responsibility to become familiar with the laws and ordinances in your community.

The Honeybee Act of 1922, passed by the US Congress, limits the import of adult, live honeybees into the US. Pests and illnesses were taken into account after an amendment in 1976. The Department of Agriculture's Secretary reaffirmed the importance of following regulations to limit the common pests and diseases that affect honeybees.

The licensing procedure is described in detail on your state's department of agriculture website. Although not all states demand a license, you must still register your beekeeping business to be inspected (to monitor insects and diseases).

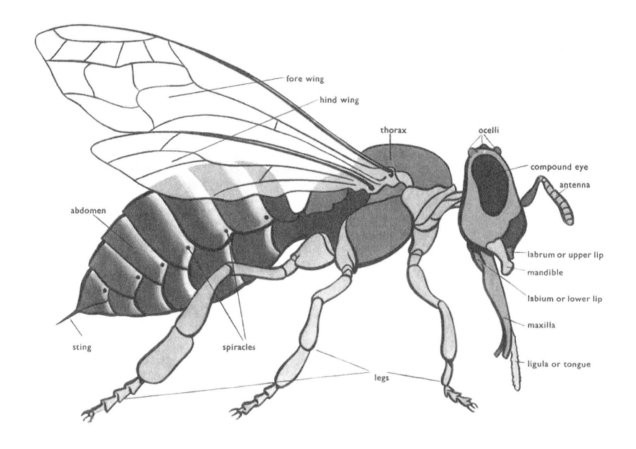

Honeybees are extremely adaptable to new enclosed settings since they are sophisticated social insects. Finding honeycombs in the open and exposed to the elements is uncommon today. Whereas honeybees establish their caste structure in the colony here, unlike in nature, we maintain them in man-made wooden hives that we either purchase or build.

For the survival of the entire colony, the complicated structure of the bee caste system needs constant movement. Let's examine the anatomy of the bee and talk about some of its fundamental physiological functions that are important for beekeeping.

Bee Anatomy

The world's most significant insect is likely the bee. It is our crops' most effective pollinator. There are more than 16,000 different species of bees, but the honeybee (Apis mellifera), is the only one that can produce honey, which is what gave it its name.

The head, thorax, and abdomen make up the honeybee's three primary body components.

energy they need to perform and produce heat. The flower the bee chooses to collect the pollen from determines its hue. Bees only select one type of pollen to gather each day.

Bees create secretions of chemicals, compounds, and pheromones through glands located all over their body. With these secretions, they combine the nectar they carry into the hive. The nectar is then fermented inside the cell for honey capping by using enzymes to help synthesize it by being thrown up into the stomachs of successively more bees. When immature honey is put in a cell for fermentation to mature and turn it into the sweet, gooey honey that we love to consume, the process is known as capping.

Let's go over the key glands of a honeybee:

1. The Nasonov gland, which is located on the upper rear abdomen, releases pheromones to guide bees in their search for food.
2. The Koschenikov gland, which is located on the lower hind abdomen, releases alarm pheromone.
3. The Dufour's gland, which is located on the lower hind abdomen, distinguishes between worker bee eggs and eggs laid by the queen (unfertilized eggs).
4. The mandibular gland, which is beneath the mandibles on the head, is where the royal jelly is made.

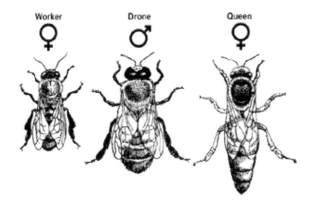

On its head, it has two antennae, a pair of mouthparts, three pairs of legs, two pairs of wings, and an abdomen with mainly black and yellow stripes surrounding the stomach and bee blood. On the thorax, it has two pairs of wings and three pairs of legs (haemolymph).

Through UV light, its complex eyes can process millions of images every minute. Insects do not smell through their breathing organ, which is located on their abdomen, but rather through their antennae. Bees have mandibles that are used to form and cut cell wax as well as cut through food and other materials.

Their proboscis serves as their primary means of ingesting nectar. To access the deeper regions of the nectaries that contain nectar in the flower, the proboscis, which resembles a tongue, elongates. Bee hair attracts pollen. Honeybees typically use their hind legs to crush pollen packets as they return to the hive. Beebread requires pollen to be made.
Let's distinguish between nectar, pollen, and honey. Bees create honey, a semi-liquid substance, from nectar. Nectar is a clear, sweet liquid that plants employ to entice pollinators like bees. They unintentionally spread pollen to other flowers because it attaches to their body.
Beebread is created when bees combine pollen and honey. The real food that the bees eat is what gives their bodies the

lower abdomen contains a wax gland that produces wax for comb drawing.

Pheromone production also involves other glands. All of the pheromones are used in bee communication.

Pheromones

Within the colony, pheromones are used to communicate critical information. There are distinctive pheromones produced by each caste and age. They instruct bees on when and how to begin their tasks. Bees are among the best-coordinated insects in nature as a result of this mechanism.

If the sender, the recipient, the communication medium, or the message itself is ineffective, bee communication will be ineffective.

The fact that bee communication will be disrupted by the rise in global temperature is one of the main causes of scientists' concern about climate change. Heat has the power to destabilize a compound or form a new one. Bees deliver erroneous messages or no messages at all when it weakens the pheromone due to its unique chemical structure being affected.

The pheromone that controls the activity of the entire colony is known as the Queen Mandibular Pheromone (QMP). It serves as a sex pheromone as well. The drones are drawn to QMP. The drones won't be able to deposit their sperm if they can't smell her fragrance. She can only be sustained for thirty minutes. If you're wondering why no eggs are being laid during the mating season, it's possible that the drones were unable to locate the queen.

The alarm pheromones that worker bees release come in two varieties: one is for defense, while the other is a repellent to ward off prospective foes. Some bees emit these alarm pheromones when you check a hive, but the smoke from a smoker hides the pheromone signal.

Bee Caste

The workers, drones, and queen make up the three adult members of the honeybee caste system. The only female bees that lay fertile eggs are the workers. All drones are male bees. The only fertile female bee and the queen is in charge of the colony. From egg to adulthood, every bee experiences the same developmental stages. Each caste has a certain function to fulfill within the hive.

Queen: Egg (3 days) Larva (8 ½ days) Capped (7 ½ days) Pupa (8 days)

Worker: Egg (3 days)   Larva (9 days)   Capped (9 days) Pupa (10/11 days)

Drone: Egg (3 days)   Larva (9 ½ days) Capped (10 ½ days)

Pupa (10 days)

Rearing refers to the process of developing an egg into a larva and a larva into a pupa so that the young bee may carry out its function in the hive. Each caste goes through distinct developmental stages and has varied nutritional needs while it is a larva.

The beginning of a bee's life is as an egg. It then transforms into a larva, an insect's larval stage that resembles a worm. The larva progresses through the pupal stage, during which the developing creature becomes dormant inside a cocoon. It changes within and comes out as a young adult bee.

It's crucial for a beginning beekeeper to understand how the hive castes differ in terms of outward appearance. Without the other castes, none of them can exist. Like any other living thing, bees have an innate will to live in order to reproduce. Even if bees are unaware of their importance to humans, we should still be grateful for what they provide for us.

Queen

In the colony, a queen is in charge of generating fertilized (female) and unfertilized (male) eggs that develop into workers, drones, and even new queens. She delegates the majority of the colony's operations using her communicative pheromone because she is the only fertile female bee in the hive (QMP). As a result, she becomes the most significant bee in the hive.

She begins her life as a fertilized female egg put atop a unique brood cell known as a "queen cup." The elongated cup protrudes from the regular waxed cells. She then develops into a larva and floats on royal jelly-water mixtures.

All female bees can be identified by their larval stage. All larvae consume both honey and royal jelly, but a queen larva only consumes the latter. This jelly aids in her physiological differentiation and aids in her development into a bee capable of depositing both fertilized and unfertilized eggs.

Sixteen days after being laid in her queen cell by the previous queen, the queen bee emerges as an adult. She then defeats rival young queen contenders to win the title. A queen bee's outward appearance makes her instantly recognizable. Her body is longer and more slender than the others, and her wings extend to the tips of her abdomen as opposed to the workers' and drones', whose wings only cover around two-thirds of it.

She cannot fit through the queen excluder, which was made to only fit worker bees, because she is larger than the other female bees. One week after emerging, she begins mating. Usually, in the afternoon, she flies out of the hive,

accompanied by numerous drones who have picked up on her scent. All she needs to lay fertilized eggs are three to eight billion sperm in her spermatheca.

She can produce 1,000 to 1,500 eggs each day, especially during the spring and summer months when demand is at its highest. A bee has a 21-day lifespan on average. Egg production will stop if she passes away, and the colony will need to find a replacement quickly.

When the queen ages and stops producing eggs, workers will raise a new queen to take her place.

Supersedure is the act of appointing a queen to succeed her own mother. Depending on the situation, this process could start naturally or be forced.

Years ago, scientists believed that bee workers selected a possible queen by generously feeding her royal jelly to aid in the development of the female reproductive system. The secret to creating a queen bee was just recently found in 2015, and it involves NOT feeding the young candidate any pollen or honey.

Through her queen mandibular pheromone, the most crucial message that she sends out changes based on what she believes the hive needs. This is the reason she is referred to as the queen; without her, the hive would be completely lifeless.

The queen must first be located and marked with a neon-colored pen on her back thorax, between her wings, when you finally build your first hive. When examining your hives, you can use this to recognize her.

Drones

A male bee known as a drone is primarily concerned with mating with the queen in order to ensure genetic reproduction. Unfertilized eggs called drones persist in the brood cells longer than workers do. Unlike worker cells, which are flat, theirs contain protruding, blunt, concave-like bullets. You can use this as one method to tell worker cells from drone cells when they are still in the pupal stage.

How many eggs will be laid in the hive is decided by the queen. Worker bees can also deposit eggs, but because they are unfertilized, they will only hatch into drones. Drones play a specific job in the hive that beekeepers and scientists are not entirely aware of; they do more than just mate and consume honey.

They are not responsible for guarding the hive against other bees or insects; workers are. In fact, drones are willing to visit any hive they choose, flirt with a virgin queen, and consume the honey from the other colony. On occasion, they congregate with drones from other hives as though they were holding a meeting. There are numerous theories, but nobody is truly an expert.

Drones don't sting. They die after mating with a queen because their sexual organ and related abdominal tissues fall off. Workers drive drones out of the hive in the fall when food is limited and honey production declines to ensure a consistent supply of honey for the brood. They are brutally abandoned and allowed to perish throughout the harsh winter.

Workers

Female honeybees make up the whole workforce. They serve as the hive's skeleton. Adult workers give larvae beebread instead of merely royal jelly throughout their larval stage. After combining with honey, beebread goes through fermentation. Although they are the tiniest bees in the hive, workers account for the majority of the colony and perform most of the work. As soon as worker bees hatch from the egg, they begin to work.

Let's discuss the worker bee's life cycle:

1. Young worker bees prepare the brood cells for usage by cleaning them on days 1 and 2 after hatching from the egg. A cell must be scrupulously cleaned by a cleaner bee before a queen bee may lay an egg there. If not done properly, the queen scouts another cell, necessitating yet another round of cleaning.
2. They develop into nursing bees between days 3 and 11. After the egg hatches, these nurses begin feeding worker and drone larvae royal jelly on days 1 and 2. Later, until they pupate, these nursing bees feed them pollen-mixed water and other micronutrients. There are also what are known as advanced nurse bees. These bees' only job is to feed the queen larva royal jelly; they never add any other food mixture.
3. Wax manufacturing takes place from days 12 to 17. These worker bees, who are practically adults, use wax to create new cells and repair broken ones. They are also responsible for storing pollen and honey that older worker bees collected from areas outside the hive.
4. Worker bees have a choice on the type of work they perform in the hive starting on days 12 through 16 and forward. There are groups who will work on all or most of the activities inside the hive, and there are groups who will work on specialized jobs.

Here are some of the duties performed by worker bees:

a) Foraging: Foragers search the surroundings for nectars and pollen that they can use to make honey. Bees drink nectar from blossoms using their proboscis. To drink nectar and gather pollen, they travel up to 5 kilometers in any direction. To create propolis, some employees gather resinous materials (from tree buds and plant/insect saps) at specific times of the day. Propolis is a glue-like material that worker bees use for a variety of purposes. Every morning, or at a time of day when the blooms are in full bloom, foragers venture out into the flora in groups.

Some groups bring in water. Bees might fly inside your home, particularly the kitchen where there is water, if there is a water shortage during the summer. If your water trough is empty and has to be filled, it is a sign.

b) Landing for orientation: The best way for a bee to find food in your neighborhood is to become familiar with it. A bee scout, whose responsibility it is to search for potential food sources, informs her of this. To show the other bees where and how she found the food supply, the scout bee performs a dance in front of them.

The bee scout returns to the hive and dances around if the food is 50 to 150 meters away. She waggles her wings in a straight line and vibrates after that. After the number "8," she says it again. She can determine where the sun is if she walks straight while following a line. The direction is right, facing the sun, if she waggles to the right. When facing the sun, she turns left if it is to the left.

c) Propolizing: This is how propolis is produced and secreted. Propolis is the bee glue that honeybees create by combining saliva and wax. It is used to cover any unwelcome openings in the hive or to hide it from outside threats. Some beekeepers dislike it when bees propolish in areas like the gaps between frames, covers, and body sides. It makes it difficult to separate one frame from another and open the hive.

We once accidentally tipped the hive over since we weren't attentive when opening the hive and used too much effort to separate the coverings. It went horribly. Propolizing is crucial for regulating the hive's temperature while being annoying. The hive maintains a more even temperature during the winter the more holes are covered. They propolish a carcass to reduce its infectious potential if the corpse is too large to be hauled outside.

d) Cleaning: Regular hive cleaning is done by a worker. To ensure that no bacteria may thrive and spread diseases in the hive, she eliminates dead bees and discarded larvae. Bees are highly particular about cleanliness; unless they are ill, you will never find a speck of dirt inside one of their hives.

Due to the pupal cocoon that is still inside after three to five broodings, the comb turns dark to black. To make sure that germs are not waiting for an opportunity to attack, it is preferable to have it updated.

e) Sealing: In the production of honey, honey sealers are essential. A bee should be able to predict when to seal a cell with honey substances. Before being sealed, honey must mature and become sufficiently dry and sticky. They must use their wings to fan the area with air to dry it if it is a little damp. Bees will chew off the cover of honey and consume the substance inside when they are hungry.

f) Feeding: With the exception of mature drones, worker bees feed the entire colony. One exception are drone larvae. Even when fully grown, worker bees still provide royal jelly to the queen. The bees that are keeping an eye out for the queen also assist in spreading QMP by fanning the hive.

g) Nursing: Nurse bees are in charge of raising new larvae. Depending on the needs of the larvae, the workers will bring food to them in three to four days. Later, the cells are sealed to prepare for the pupal stage. The nurse bees can tell whether they are working on a worker, drone, or queen cell by smelling the pheromone that a larva secretes.

h) Building: Using wax produced by other worker bees, worker bees draw the comb (young adult bees). It requires a lot of effort and wax to construct combs. Give the hive particular attention during winterization if bees are unable to construct comb in the late summer.

i) Guarding: Guard bees keep an eye out for trespassers like wasps, other insects, and rodents near the hive's entrance. They use their sense of smell to examine everything that enters the hive, including foragers bringing in pollen. When in a protective position, a guard bee will stand on her four hind legs. To assess the situation, she raises her antennae straight up; if it is too much to handle, she activates the alarm pheromone for support. Everyone tackles the intruder as soon as help arrives, which is always within seconds.

j) Robbing: In order to obtain honey, bees also rob other colonies. It can occur at any time and is a significant issue in the fall, but it is controllable. Stronger colonies feed off of weaker hives, particularly if they are broken. Bees do this naturally. Stronger colonies will raid other hives for food if your area has few nectar sources.
We once inserted a weak super with half-filled honey frames in error, expecting the previous colony would accept them. Within hours, there was a robbery, and the super was quickly honey-emptied. Each colony's mortality rate was high. The fact that worker bees don't always accept bees from neighboring hives should be considered.

The caliber of pheromone the queen distributes to the colony affects the actions in the hive. The condition of your hive is based on the status of the queen. The choice of the queen, however, and whether or not she is a good fit for the hive are made by the workers. The colony's bees cooperate with one another to promote growth.

The Brood

The egg resembles a very small grain of white rice. The egg stands straight up in the cage for three days after the queen places it there. Hold the frame up to the sun to reveal the eggs, which appear as silhouettes of grains inside the frame. The queen begins the brood in the center and moves outward from there. This is what we refer to as the laying pattern, and it will have various management consequences for beehives.

Either a single or double brood box may be used. By adding a second deep super and frames for the bees to work on, you double the brood box. Newer supers that have been put on top of the main body typically have lighter combs because only honey is kept inside, but the frame combs in the main body are darker because they have been brooded a few times. Darker combs will make it more difficult to find eggs. About every four to five years, we clean the frames.

The larval phase of the bee begins when it is still an egg and grows into a grub.

For a total of six days on average, five nurse bees feed each worker and drone larva 100 times every day. They bob up and down in bee milk, water, and honey as they curl up like the letter "C." The adult workers cover the larva's cells after six days, during which time the larva weaves a cocoon to prepare for the pupal stage.

The pupal stage lasts 12 days for new workers, 14 1/2 days for drones, and 7 1/2 days for new queens. The pupa starts to resemble an adult during these days, starting with the color of its eyes, which change from white to brown or purple. The entire organism follows, which emerges from the cell and begins to clean itself, then it's off to work as a young adult bee.

Chapter 6
Where Do You Get Bees?

It's fantastic that you have everything you need to set up your beehive, but what about the bees? You may start your colony using a few different strategies, and we'll go over some of the simplest ones below!

Before proceeding, we must first respond to the following important query:

When Should You Populate Your Beehive?

The spring is the ideal time to populate your beehive.

Depending on where you are on the planet, this might begin around April. But because beekeeping is a well-liked hobby lately, we advise acquiring your bees as early as January to make sure your colony gets started on schedule. There may occasionally be a backlog, and clearing it up could take months.

Please continue reading to learn about our suggested beehive populating techniques.

HONEYBEE PACKAGES

One isolated, artificially inseminated queen bee and about 10,000 worker bees are contained in a box called a honeybee package. These packets, which are suitable for quickly and successfully stocking any hive, are available directly from bee breeders. Due to their simplicity of usage, these packages frequently sell out, so be sure you have good connections to apiaries (locations where bees are housed) in your neighborhood so you can obtain a package when you need it.

If you're unsure, a quick Google search for "bee packages" should clear things up.

Just make sure the source you're using is trustworthy and engages in ethical beekeeping.

How to Install a Honey Bee Package

Within one or two days of receiving your bee package, you must install it. Remove the queen from the box first, then install it (keeping her in her cage). The queen bee cage should be attached right next to the syrup tin inside the box. To remove the queen, first knock the bee package on the ground to cause all the bees to fall to the bottom, remove the sugar syrup can from the top, quickly grab the queen bee cage, and quickly replace the sugar syrup can to prevent your bees from escaping.

The bees will gnaw through the hard candy used to close the queen bee cage, allowing the queen to escape. By performing this ritual, the queen decreases the likelihood that the colony would reject her by giving the worker bees time to get used to her fragrance. It is advised that you poke a hole in the candy with a sharp point to start the bees, but you must take great care to avoid accidentally releasing or harming the bees. If you're working with a top-bar hive, place the queen cage toward the bottom of the hive cavity.

Tap the package on the ground once more to get all of your bees away from the top entrance and into the hive. Remove the can of sugar syrup, then quickly deposit the bees into the hive. Try to remove as many as you can by gently shaking the box side to side. Once you're satisfied, lean the package's entrance against the beehive entrance and let the bees enter at their own rate. A few resistant bees may still remain in the package.

You're all set once you replace your hive's ceiling and bars.

Extra: When placing your bees in the hive, it's a good idea to prepare a sugar water solution to aid in the honeycomb-building process.

NUCLEUS BOXES

Essentially a small beehive, a nucleus box, is often known as a "nuc." It's frequently a wooden box with three to five frames of honey and brood (bee eggs, larvae, and pupae), one queen bee, and enough worker bees to establish/expand a new hive.

Nuc boxes are readily available from apiaries and bee breeders. In terms of population management, a nucleus box might be preferable to a bee package because the bees will already have some eggs, honey reserves, and larvae on hand. By using a nuc box, they won't have to start from scratch, which will allow them to construct the hive much more quickly.

An empty nuc box is an excellent alternative for a temporary swarm trap once you've moved the contents of your old hive into your new one (see next section). The process will be a little bit simpler and less stressful if you catch a swarm in a nuc box. You can leave the swarm there for a time so that it can begin to construct a honeycomb rather than moving it into a new hive right away.

SWARMING

Swarming is the most organic way to populate beehives since it makes use of a phenomenon that happens very naturally. The old queen is replaced by a colony, and the new queen swarms out of the hive with about half of the hive and some honey. These swarms will land on a building near the original hive, and "scout bees" will depart the swarm to find a better place for them to establish their new permanent hive. The swarm can be captured during this time and used to populate a new hive. These swarms are easily adaptable to new hives and will be prepared to begin making honeycomb almost immediately. This strategy works well for assuring strong genetics among the local bee population because swarms are native to the region in which they will be located. They'll likely do better than bee colonies that have been relocated across the country as well (as bee packages or nuc boxes sometimes are). The beehive may be easily captured using this technique, making it the least expensive means of populating a beehive (read below to find out how).

Swarming is an excellent way to populate hives; however, it should be noted that swarms must be discovered spontaneously, thus they are not a reliable source of bees (like bee packages are).

How to Catch and Install a Swarm

Make sure your beekeeping supplies are ready before beginning anything. You'll require the following in order to capture a swarm:

- a cardboard box (or nucleus box)
- a ladder or stool (if necessary)
- a bee brush
- a light-colored bed sheet (or tarp)
- protective gear
- pruning shears
- tape
- lemongrass oil

CATCHING A SWARM

When you have located a swarm that you believe you can safely catch, put on your safety gear, lay out your sheet or tarp below it, and then place your box on top of it. Start by trying to fit as much of the swarm as you can inside the box (using gloved hands or a bee brush). To induce the bees to descend inside the box, if your swarm is perched on a tree, gently shake the limb. If your bees leave the box, it's likely that the queen didn't accompany them. If this occurs, wait a few minutes for the bees to re-cluster around the queen before attempting again.

Using your pruning shears, cut the branch from the tree or bush where the cluster is located, then place it in the box with the swarm. Just make sure to clear out all the branches and plants before putting the swarm inside the hive. Try lightly spraying them with water and brushing them into the box if the swarm is on a wall or another difficult-to-navigate surface. They find it harder to fly away because of the water. If your cluster is on the ground, all you need to do is put some lemongrass oil inside the box and tip it so the cluster may crawl inside. Bees are drawn to lemongrass oil.

INSTALLING A SWARM INTO A NEW HIVE

Once the majority of the bees are inside, seal the box while leaving a tiny opening for any scout bees or leftover bees. To give scout bees ample time to complete their rounds, make sure to leave the box there until the sun sets. At night, tape the box shut entirely and cover the swarm with a bed sheet or tarp. Air holes must be present. The following morning, be very cautious when moving the swarm box and setting them up in their new hive. Open the package when you're ready, then shake the bees into the hive. Reinstall the bars and lid to complete the task.

Swarm traps can be put up to encourage swarming. These function best when placed high up, as in a tree. If you add a few drops of lemongrass oil to these traps, swarms will be drawn in.

BAIT AND TRAP

Read the information on swarming above before reading this section because baiting and trapping is a technique that extends swarming. The scout bees will depart the swarm to look for a new suitable hive location, as you are aware from prior experience when swarms form on their "temporary" new base. They return to the hive after finding one and use a unique dance to guide the bees to the new location.

To make it simpler for the other bees to follow them, a few worker bees fly to the new place and produce a pheromone that smells exactly like—you got it—lemongrass oil. Lemongrass oil is an excellent enticement to bring bees to a spot, as was previously noted. Therefore, apply a small drop of the oil—don't use too much!—and let it do its magic to attract bees to the swarm trap.

SPLITTING

Hive splitting occurs when a beekeeper merely moves the hive's frames (or top bars) into a new hive, "dividing" an existing hive in to two. Unhatched eggs, nursing bees, and honey from the preceding colony ought to be present on these frames/top bars. The worker bees can raise a new queen bee by feeding an unhatched egg royal jelly if the bar or frames you remove don't already contain one, so don't worry too much.

It is crucial that your frames and bars include unhatched eggs because this process cannot take place if the egg has already hatched. Of course, you could just buy queen bees and add them one at a time, but most beekeepers seem to favor the custom of adding queens spontaneously to hives.

Do your research to determine whether a queen bee has been raised responsibly before purchasing it because the methods used to inseminate queen bees can be problematic. You only need to take a frame or bar out of one hive and put it in the next one to add a "split" to it. It's ridiculously easy.

These days, splitting is a preferred method for populating new hives because it is a simple, natural option that maximizes the use of an existing bee colony. Since you only require an established colony, it is also totally free. Why not try to make some new beekeeper friends and work out an arrangement to split one of their current hives with them if you're just starting out?

THE LANGSTROTH HIVE

When you mention beekeeping, most people picture the box with stacked layers as a beehive, known as a Langstroth hive. LL Langstroth, a minister, built this beehive in 1852.

The main idea of Langstroth is that it is simple to use, expand, and access. The introduction of vertically hanging frames was this hive's ground-breaking innovation.

Additionally, this design made sure that there would be at least a 1/4" space between each frame, providing enough room for bees.

A Langstroth hive can be expanded by simply adding a new layer.

The fact that the Langstroth hive's dimensions are essentially universally standardized is another major benefit. As a result, you shouldn't encounter too many problems with inconsistent sizing if you purchase parts for the hive from different vendors.

THE WARRE HIVE

In terms of form and layout, the Warre hive is somewhat similar to the Langstroth. This hive was designed in accordance with the bees' natural habitat by a French monk by the name of Abbé Émile Warré. Because of this, many wild bees opt to construct their colony in a hollow tree, which is similar to the inside of a Warre hive.

A Warre hive differs significantly from a Langstroth hive in that additional boxes are added beneath the current boxes. They take first place with the Langstroth. Furthermore, the Warre boxes are often a little lighter and smaller.

Another distinction is that the Warre hive frequently does not have foundations, allowing bees to organically build vertically branching comb.

Condensation is another thing bees particularly dislike, and

Beehives

There are many various types of beehives available, and each beekeeper may choose a particular variety depending on their location, regional climate, or preferred maintenance method.

We'll go through each of the three widely used options—the Langstroth, the Top-Bar, and the Warre—along with some of their benefits in this section.

There is no good solution, as there are always advantages and disadvantages to consider. Before deciding which is best for you, give them careful thought. The most crucial thing to keep in mind is that there is no right or wrong way to do anything.

Let's start by taking a look at the Langstroth hive.

the Warre hive's ceiling (quilt box) is superb at absorbing it.

It requires less upkeep overall, which could appeal to novice beekeepers.

THE TOP-BAR HIVE

The top bar is entirely unique from the others in terms of design. Instead of a stacked, tiered design, it has a straightforward "bathtub"-like shape with frames running along it.

The top-bar hive's benefits include a significantly simpler overall structure and much easier access to the frames. The top-bar hive doesn't require as many elements as a regular hive, as you'll see in the following section. It is very straightforward and simple to use. Like the Warre hive, because it has no foundations, it resembles the natural environment of bees.

The Elements of a Beehive

THE BASIC SET-UP

The beehive, as we previously mentioned, is a very complicated structure with many parts intended to keep the bees happy and increase their honey production as much as possible. It is not simply a wooden box with a few frames inside. Most contemporary designs also prioritize usability and safety. It is far preferable to have a beehive that makes honey harvesting simple and secure as opposed to one that makes it challenging and stressful.

It can be quite intimidating for a novice beekeeper to look at a hive, so let's break down all the many parts that are often found in a beehive.

There are still many distinct types of beehives used frequently in beekeeping. The good thing is that they all work similarly, so they essentially have the same internal structure.

THE HIVE SET-UP

The layers of a typical beehive are as follows (starting at the point at the top of the list and working down as a real beehive would):

OUTER COVER

The outer cover, which is frequently referred to as the "telescoping cover," serves as the hive's roof. It's crucial to safeguard your hive from adverse weather so that the bees within can survive. A sort of metal sheet (such as aluminum, zinc, steel, or copper) is typically placed on top of flat, outside covers to provide additional protection from the elements. Even while the outer cover's composition matters, it is crucial to make sure that it is broader than the actual

hive to protect the entire structure. For further security, the outer cover should be able to fit over the inner cover's edge.

FEEDERS

Feeders are crucial because they provide food for your worker bees when there isn't enough extra honey to go around. Even bees, despite their intelligence and productivity, occasionally require assistance. There are several different kinds of feeders; some are fastened to the hive entrance, others are inserted between the hive's frames, and still, others are simply left outdoors in a careless manner. Which type you choose depends on your particular preferences.

The fact that interior feeders are less appealing to robber bees and other similar predators is a major benefit of having them.

Additionally, having a food supply that they can access inside of their hive is far more comfortable for your bees.

If you're installing your feeder internally, it must be placed right above the brood box so that the bees may easily access it. The queen excluder layer must be removed, though, as doing so will make it more difficult for the bees to get to it.

Internal hive top feeders are one popular kind of feeder. These are useful since they can carry a lot of sugar syrup and even include unique accessories that stop the bees from drowning if they accidentally fall into the syrup. When you need to feed a sizable colony of bees from a single source, this kind of feeder is ideal.

Another feeder option is similar to the previous one, but it is an exterior hive top feeder. Usually, sugar syrup-filled plastic or Mason jars are used to make these feeders. These containers are usually encircled by a straightforward empty hive box and are flipped upside down over the entrance hole of the inner cover. This solution is useful for shielding the syrup from inclement weather and thieving bees.

A feeding shim is one more example of a frequently used feeder. A feeding shim is a hive-sized empty wooden box stocked with feeding utensils. These are well-liked options for giving sugar candy to bees throughout the coldest months of the year.

INNER COVER

The hive's ceiling is essentially the inside cover. It has an entry notch at the front and a second entrance hole in the center. This entry needs to be facing forward when the cover is being installed. The openings stated above are quite significant because they guarantee that the hive can maintain proper ventilation. The bees might utilize these pores as an escape route while you're extracting honey or injecting feeders into the hive.

The best inner cover is one constructed of plywood because other types will sag over time, which is terrible if you're trying to save room inside your hive.

Be careful when doing this because it's very simple for folks to install their inner coverings wrong. The "summer" and "winter" positions of inner covers are known; for the majority of the year, your covers should be in the "summer" position. The cover features a flat surface on one side and a frame with a little open area on the other side. The flat side of the cover should be facing down, and the framed side should be facing up, in order to position it for summer use. The inner and outer covers are separated by an air gap in this configuration, which helps to keep the hive a little bit cooler.

HONEY SUPERS

The layer located above the queen excluder and brood boxes is known as the honey super. Your bees will work furiously to create honey, which will be stored in this layer. Super boxes are normally smaller than the actual brood box and typically come in two sizes: medium and shallow.

Smaller honey supers will likely be filled with honey more evenly by your bees, although medium-sized supers are the most typical.

You will extract honey from your hives by taking it out of the supers when the time arrives. Do not forget to leave your bees with enough honey to last them through the winter.

QUEEN EXCLUDER

The layer known as the queen excluder aids in dividing the hive into two crucial sections: the one where honey is kept and the one where eggs are placed. It goes without saying that you shouldn't combine the two. The queen excluder is a type of mesh that rests on top of the brood box and is too narrow for the queen to pass through (hence the name). The queen cannot lay eggs in the honey supers because it prohibits her from accessing them. Queen excluders are available in a variety of materials including metal, plastic, wood, etc.

Actually, some beekeepers disagree with the use of queen excluders. Some believe this layer to be a required protocol for maintaining a well-organized and effective hive, while others believe it to be superfluous because it appears to stress the worker bees (who dislike having to squeeze through tiny spaces and don't like to move around without the queen). However, since the methods you'll need to employ to prevent using a queen excluder are a little more difficult, we'd strongly advise employing one if you're a newbie.

FRAMES

Every single kind of beehive makes use of a frame in some way. A beehive without frames isn't one, period. The shape of a beehive's frame varies depending on the type of hive, but it is always present in some way.

On top of the frame, the bees will build their honeycomb. "Drawing comb" is how beekeepers refer to the process of creating honeycomb.

A " foundation" sheet, which is essentially a hexagonal pattern created out of pressed wax or plastic, is frequently attached to frames. This design serves as a foundation for the bees to build their honeycomb, making the finished product neater and more organized. A foundation sheet is obviously not a necessity, and some beekeepers prefer not to use them at all. The term "foundationless frames" is aptly used to describe frames without a foundation.

The actual frames are normally constructed of wood; however, beekeepers occasionally use plastic. The size of the frame you use must, of course, correspond to the size of your hive. There are three sizes of frames: shallow, medium, and deep. Due to the necessity for them to be a little larger, "deep" frames are typically found in brood boxes. While honey supers of the same size are most frequently utilized with shallow and medium frames.

The majority of frames available for purchase on the market have comparable sizes, but not all brands will be exactly the same. Before making a purchase, make sure the frames will fit into the hive you already own or wish to acquire.

Use identically sized/typed frames inside one hive to avoid problems with bee space compromise (see next section for more information on bee space).

BROOD BOX

The "brood," also known as the region where the queen lays her eggs, is located in the brood box, which is the lowest box in the hive. Additionally, the queen resides there. Given that it must handle the bee colony's expansion throughout the relevant season, the brood box should be the largest component of the hive. A second brood box can be installed to provide more room if the first one is insufficient.

Bees use several frames called brood boxes to make wax comb. The type of hive you have determines how many frames the brood box has (it will probably be around eight or ten). Ten frames are acceptable if you don't mind the extra weight, but if you must transport your hive for some reason, be careful to consider this since a 10-frame brood box can

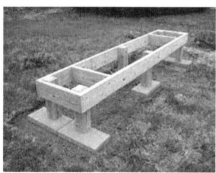

become quite heavy very soon. Fewer frames are desirable for a lighter hive. A 10-frame box might be preferable if your first objective is to increase your colony's size and generate as much honey as possible.

Extra: There are several terms used to describe brood boxes such as "brood chamber," "deep hive body," and even "deep supers" or "brood supers." However, the word "super" in the name has the potential to mislead new beekeepers; therefore, it is crucial to distinguish between the honey

supers and the brood boxes, which are two distinct yet equally vital components. Above the brood boxes, and separated from them by a queen excluder, should be the super honey layer. Do not confuse them!

This component of the hive is optional, but many beekeepers strongly recommend utilizing them, so it depends on your preferences. A slatted rack, also known as a brood rack, is a component of a hive that aids in avoiding problems with ventilation or congestion. It may feel a little congested when your hive is at its busiest point during the peak of the season! The bees have a little more room to roam around below the brood box when using a slatted rack. It's ideal for keeping your hive well-ventilated and avoiding congestion. Adding more room with a slatted rack also aids in keeping your hive warmer in the winter.

Make sure you install a slatted rack correctly if you wish to utilize one. The shallow side of a slatted rack, which has a deep and shallow side, should be positioned upward and parallel to the frames of your brood box. It will be a bit more difficult for you to manage and remove your brood box frames if you don't arrange it this way since the bees will probably fill the extra space with burr comb.

ENTRANCE REDUCER

The purpose of the entrance reducer is to essentially minimize the size of the hive entrance. This component, which fits tightly between the bottom board and the bottom hive box, is particularly helpful for restricting entry into the hive. They can also be utilized to keep other pests out of your hive. Having a small entry space enables bees to defend the hive more effectively in the event that it is "robbed" by predators.

The entrance reducer is an extended piece of wood with numerous entrances of various sizes. To alter the size of the entrance to the hive, the wood is turned.

The key piece of advice we can offer when purchasing this piece of equipment is to purchase an entrance reducer from the same supplier as your other hive components. This is to prevent disappointment because different brands' size ranges aren't always accurate.

BOTTOM BOARD

Essentially, the hive's floor is the bottom board. Here are the following two types of bottom boards:

Screened: A bottom board with a mesh screen, usually composed of wire or plastic, is excellent for ventilation. It can help reduce humidity and maintain a comfortable temperature inside the hive. This screen board is also believed to be more effective at defending the hive from pests like moths or varroa (a sort of mite that can greatly disrupt beehives). Due to the gaps in the screen, objects can fall through them, which can also help keep the hive a little cleaner.

A tray of some sort that can be slid shut to seal the bottom of the hive will be included with a bottom board with a screened mesh of excellent quality. This is helpful when it's freezing outside or you want to check on the hive.

Solid: As you might anticipate, a solid bottom board is one that is free of holes. This style has the advantage of keeping the bottom of the hive significantly warmer in colder weather, and ventilation can be drastically restricted. Bees will be encouraged to begin working (or brood rearing) earlier in the day as a result of the warmer hive. This type of board will catch a lot of different garbage because solid bottom boards don't have gaps where trash and other items could fall through. As a result, a solid bottom board requires routine cleaning.

HIVE STAND

The hive stand, which is the framework on top of which the entire hive will be placed, is an essential component of the hive setup for a variety of reasons. It prevents unwelcome moisture from getting into the hive. Because bees hate wetness and prefer to avoid humidity as much as possible, wild beehives are often found in trees or at the highest possible elevation. In fact, if a hive receives too much moisture, a bee colony may perish.

You'll find it simpler to maintain your colony if you use a hive stand, which is still another important benefit. Having a raised hive base will make life much easier because bending over to complete all the bee-related duties can hurt your back.

There are two different kinds of hive stands you can purchase: single and multiple. While beekeepers frequently construct numerous hive supports themselves, single hive stands are frequently purchased commercially. The biggest advantage of having a multiple hive stand is that there will be enough space between hives for inspection. Inspection necessitates disassembling your hive, and you'll need space to lay the parts down. These types of hive stands can be constructed with cement blocks or timber beams.

Just keep in mind that a stand for several hives needs to be strong enough to handle a lot of weight and to be as level as possible with the ground.

Although you can purchase one that you can easily install, building single hive supports is also an option. A single hive stand is far more forgiving and can be readily stabilized even while working with uneven terrain. Just be sure to purchase a hive stand that is the appropriate size for your hive (depending on whether it is an 8- or 10-frame hive). Depending on the model of hive stand you buy, some can include an extra landing board, which functions as a kind of ramp for bees entering and exiting the hive. Most people concur that a landing board is a good piece of extra gear for

beginning beekeepers since it allows them to monitor the colony before it disappears into the hive. Simple observation for a few minutes can teach you a lot about the routines and behaviors of bees!

However, landing boards are not important pieces of equipment to have because they are not required for the bees' everyday activities. In fact, according to scientists, these boards may prevent honeybees from surviving in some regions. These ramps can also be an issue in certain weather circumstances because, for example, if it snows, the entrance may become blocked, or if it rains, bees may become entangled in it.

Considering Bee Space

Modern beehives are made to be safe and simple to use, but they are also made to accommodate how bees like to move around the hive in order to assure their comfort and security— otherwise known as bee space! Bee space was already stated in the part above, but here we'll go over why it's so crucial and provide additional details on what it is specifically.

Bee space is the amount of unoccupied area inside the hive that bees can use to move around and do their tasks. It's a space of typically around 1 centimeter that the bees won't encrust with honeycomb, allowing them to move freely.

Although bee space might appear minor, it is crucial to ensure that bees can function properly. It's crucial to take into account this area while building a beehive since it fulfills a very helpful secondary purpose by providing a small opening where we may remove the hive without destroying the honeycomb.

LANGSTROTH BEE HIVE

The Langstroth hive was the first hive design to take into account "bee space" (see the above picture). Even now, one of the most preferred designs for beekeepers is the Langstroth hive.

Bees will build burr comb to fill the empty space in the hive if bee space is ignored or too much is left. This is another reason why bee space is so crucial. Due to the burr comb's haphazard construction, it can soon become untidy and make removing individual hive components much more challenging. Regularly checking the hives for unwanted burr comb and removing it (CAREFULLY) if detected are the best ways to deal with it.

Burr comb is commonly used by the queen to lay eggs; therefore, you should be very careful when looking for it in your hive. If you remove the burr comb, you can unintentionally remove the queen from the hive. Before taking anything out of the hive or discarding it, make sure to inspect it carefully and thoroughly.

There are numerous things to consider while choosing the optimal location for your apiary! It cannot be thrown around and hoped for the best. The requirements of your bee colony, your comfort, and the kind of honey you wish to produce should all be taken into account when determining the optimal site for you and your bees. The distinction between a good and a terrible location could be substantial.

Now, we're going to discuss some location-related aspects in this section:

Where is a Bee's Natural Habitat?

It's crucial to take the bees' native habitat into account when growing a bee colony since we want to resemble it as closely as possible. Bees create hives naturally in trees, ideally between a wooded area and a flower field. This gives them security, keeps them dry and protected, and makes it simple for them to access pollen.

We need to pay attention to these things to keep our bees content and productive when moving them into a hive (moving them from natural habitat to a man-made one, for example).

SOUTHEAST FACING ENTRANCE (ACCORDING TO YOUR LOCATION)

Bees don't really care whether the entrance to their hive faces southeast, yet doing so has several advantages.

The morning sun rises from the south or southeast, depending on where you are located, which is the first reason. As bees won't start working until the hive heats up, facing your hive toward the dawn will increase your bees' productivity in the morning. They can start their day with a bit of warmth from the morning sun.

The second reason is that, depending on your location, the northwest is often where the strongest winds originate. Your bees won't have to contend with cooler temperatures and excessive ventilation if you face the entrance away from that breeze. Additionally, when they are not forced to battle gales, your bees will be able to leave the hive much more easily.

Let's say you're not sure which way is the ideal place for your beehive entrance in your neighborhood. In that case, it might be wise to get in touch with your neighborhood bee group to find out what local beekeepers often do. Alternatively, if you have any friends who maintain bees, feel free to ask them!

WIND

Typically, bees select locations for their hives that are sturdy and wind-protected (within tree trunks, for example), as they do not want their hive to be harmed or blown away.

Being blown over is the last thing you want, especially if you have multiple bee boxes stacked together.

Decide where your hive will be located so that it will be adequately shielded from strong winds, or think about building a wind barrier. After determining the direction the wind is most likely to come from where you are, think about positioning your hive behind a building, a wall, a large tree, etc. If you don't have any of the aforementioned materials, you can improvise a structure out of a fence, tarp, etc.

Winter is a crucial time to take wind into account because winter winds may be incredibly destructive. Use a strong bottom board in your hive to reduce the amount of wind exposure there is throughout the winter.

SUNLIGHT

Finding exactly how much sunlight a hive requires can be a little challenging for beekeepers. The general belief is that sunshine is beneficial. However, bees normally favor a cooler, shadier environment for their hives. Bees prioritize comfort and safety above all else, therefore even though they work more efficiently in the sunshine, they don't give it much thought when choosing the ideal location for their hive.

However, positioning hives in the shade has downsides. They are more susceptible to problems including mildew, hive beetle infestation, illnesses, and other pests. Exposure to direct sunshine can oftentimes resolve or prevent many of these problems.

As a result, the majority of experts actually advise placing your hive in a location that receives direct sunshine. But it really does depend on your region's climate. It's generally best to provide your hive with some shade if you live somewhere where the temperature rises quite a bit (like the south and southwest of the US). As much as you can, try to keep your bees from overheating.

When your bees engage in specific behaviors like bearding or fanning, the hive is overheated. This interferes with their output and may harm the bees as well as the hive.

FOOD

The closer, the better when it comes to eating. If they must, bees will journey up to 6 miles in search of food.

A FEW ADDITIONAL POINTS ARE WORTH MENTIONING:

If there is a nearby farm that you want your bees to pollinate, make sure the farmer doesn't use pesticides. It is best to avoid pesticides wherever possible because they can harm bees in a variety of ways.

You don't need to locate your beehives immediately next to a garden if you want your bees to pollinate it. A garden that frequently has people walking through it is not a good place for happy bees since you should avoid areas with heavy foot activity.

WATER

Like most other animals, bees require water! A beehive can consume a full gallon of water during hot weather. Contrary to popular belief, bees only really consume honey throughout the winter to provide them with extra energy. Although bees are excellent at discovering water sources, you should place your hives close by one to ease their lives and maximize their productivity.

If possible, building a pond close to your beehives would be a fantastic water source for them. Just keep in mind that since bees cannot swim, placing your hive close to a deep water source may be dangerous. It's preferable to offer a shallow drinking source or one with rocks or pebbles so they can stand on them while drinking.

DRY GROUND

Moisture is the major thing that bees detest. It is therefore crucial to locate your hive in a dry area. If you live in an area where it frequently rains, this is something you should pay particular attention to. It might sink the dirt and cause your hive to be uneven, which can stop your bees from producing a comb and result in an uneven or messy comb.

Additionally, as beehives may be quite hefty, it's a good idea to stay away from "marshy" land while installing your beehive! The weight of a normal hive might easily exceed 100 pounds.

If there aren't any "dry ground" patches available in your location and it frequently rains, create some on your own. To set up your hive, you might have a small area with stones, decking, or pavement.

FLAT LAND

We briefly discussed this in the last point, but now we're concentrating on terrain with natural elevation like hills and valleys.

The main issue with placing your hive in a valley is that a lot of chilly air will inevitably pass through it.

Another issue with positioning hives in terrains like valleys or hills is that, in the event that you need to transfer them, it becomes quite difficult. When packed with honey, a medium-sized hive can weigh a substantial 60 pounds, which is a lot of weight to transport up and down a hill.

LOW FOOT TRAFFIC

As we've previously mentioned, it's best to locate your hive in a place where there aren't many people hanging out. It's not a good idea to place your apiary close to a place where kids play, cars frequently pass, etc. since bees typically prefer to be in hives in remote regions.

Because of this, placing hives too close to a beekeeper's residence, garden, playground, shared property boundary, etc. is frequently discouraged.

If you're unclear about what to do with the available space, just make sure your hives are at least 20 feet away from any location where humans or animals frequently enter or create noise. As we previously indicated, it's a good idea to place a tree or fence close to your hive to protect it from the wind. If you do this, make sure the entrance is not facing the object to make it easier for the bees to get in and out.

It'll just be a lot harder to garden if you have a bunch of bees buzzing around all the time, as we indicated in the "food"

part, so don't place your bees too close to it. It will hurt a little if a bee flies into you because they normally fly at a speed of 15 mph. You don't have to place bees in or close to your garden for them to find it; they will find it on their own.

Extra: You must keep track of the "kind" of honey being produced by noting the varieties of flowers your bees visit when they create honey. Some flowers' pollen actually imparts harmful properties to the honey that is manufactured from them, such as the rhododendron ponticum (a unique rhododendron that grows in Turkey), which includes the grayanotoxin in honey that, when swallowed, can cause convulsions, nausea, and dizziness. Do your research, of course!

Space Between Beehives

You should avoid placing your hives close to one another as a general rule of thumb and a matter of common sense. I'm sure you were aware of that...but did you know they need to be at least 6 feet apart?

In addition to providing you with enough room to operate on your hive and move your hive tool, this is mostly done for your bees' comfort. Use 8-frame hives (instead of 10) if you have a little less room, and make sure there is at least 3 feet between each one.

By placing your hives next to one another, there is a chance that the bees will either abscond from the hive or rob one another, taking the honey that has been stored in the other hive. Placement of the hives farther away may appear to be a rational solution to this problem, which is a prevalent dread among novice beekeepers.

No matter what you do, though, your bees will attempt to rob one another. Use an entrance reducer on your hive and set it to the shortest aperture as one method of reducing this.

Extra: How to Stop Bees Absconding

Bees may leave their hive for a number of reasons, including a shortage of food or resources, a lack of adaptation, or frequent interruptions from pests, people, wetness, etc.

The best technique to stop bees from escaping is to place a second queen excluder between the bottom board and the brood chamber. They find it more difficult to flee as a result, making them more prone to acclimate to their surroundings, which minimizes absconding. Furthermore, the queen will be unable to escape thanks to this queen excluder, and numerous bees will be reluctant to fly away without their queen. Information on queen excluders can be found in the preceding section.

When deciding where to place your new apiary, keep these points in mind.

Let's look at some tips for building your beehives before we get into the step-by-step instructions for actually putting your hive together.

General Hive Structure Advice

A top-bar hive has a straightforward design. You won't have to worry about it, as it doesn't utilize the two brood boxes and three medium-sized supers that are recommended for beginners.

If you're assembling your hive yourself from parts you've bought, it's best to avoid ordering pieces from different sources because the measurements might not be constant, and you risk having a hive that won't fit together.

The most typical material used to construct a beehive from scratch is painted pine wood.

Pinewood will decay with time as a result of exposure to the environment, therefore painting it or applying a 20:1 mixture of linseed oil and beeswax to the surface will help to increase its lifespan.

If you can find some red cedar wood, it's an excellent material to use to create a hive. It lasts a lot longer and doesn't need any paint because the wood's natural oils provide protection. However, treated pine wood is more prevalent since it is cheaper.

What is a Top-Bar Hive?

One of the first hive types used in household beekeeping, the top-bar hive was originally used in the 1600s, according to records.

Various materials are utilized to construct top-bar hives, but protected/painted wood is the most popular choice.

A top-bar hive is a long, rectangular structure that resembles a bathtub or trough in certain ways. The hive has a number of top-hung frames where the bees construct a comb that extends from the top to the bottom. Most of the time, these frames don't require a foundation because gravity helps the bees build the comb.

Because of this, the majority of people claim that the top-bar hive promotes a more genuine and natural bee environment. Beekeepers that prefer to see their hives in a setting as similar to nature as possible are known as top-bar lovers.

Top-Bar Hive Benefits

When harvesting honey, you won't need to lift large boxes or disturb your bees as much thanks to the horizontal design.

The structure of the hive is far simpler than the classic "stacked" beehive model that we previously covered. This makes it an excellent option for novices!

The combs are considerably simpler to take off, which makes life easier and makes your bees more understanding when you do. Therefore, a newbie may handle it more easily in general.

The majority of top-hive bars feature a lengthy "window" down the side that allows you to see your bees at work without disturbing them.

Building a Top-Bar Hive: Step-by-Step

You can make a 36"-long hive, and it may take almost eight hours to complete. Keep that in mind while you assemble it; this guide shows you how to create a top-bar hive from the inside out and upside down.

WHAT YOU'LL NEED FOR THIS PROJECT ARE:

12" x 1"-thick pieces of wood (or 25mm x 300mm). Simply join two 6" boards with adhesive if you can't find any 12" broad planks. If you can't get 1"-thick wood, 3/4" will do, but heavier wood will be better insulated and survive longer.

Three 12" x 36" wood pieces are required to construct a 36" hive, with one of the pieces being divided into two 18" x 12" pieces for the ends.

A piece measuring 36" x 6" or a basic mesh the same size will serve as the hive's floorboard. Despite being sliced 3" wide lengthwise, the legs will be the same size and will be cut.

For the mesh floor, you'll require a piece of plastic or stainless steel mesh with 8–10 holes spaced evenly along each inch, as well as a number of flat-headed pins to secure it to the frame (for all seasons, excluding the chilly winter months).

For the top bars, you'll also need 30 feet of 1 1/4" x 3/4" straight lumber, as well as a board that is at least 11" x 25" long.

You'll also need eight 2" (50mm) galvanized or stainless bolts with nuts and washers for the hive body, as well as twelve 2 1/2" (60mm) stainless steel or brass wood screws.

You will require clamps, a square, a screwdriver, a drill, a plane, and a carpenter's saw as tools. If available, a power drill or bench-mounted circular saw would be helpful.

For any permanent joints, you'll need strong, weatherproof exterior-grade glue. Epoxy resin glue is optional; you are not required to use it.

TO BUILD THE TOP BARS

Choosing the top bar's width is the most important aspect of the top bar hive. The majority of people advise a width between 1 1/4" and 1 3/8" (32-35mm). If you consult local authorities and they advise doing something different, heed their advice. Trial and error may be necessary; if you build the hive and discover that your bees need additional room, make the following set of bars accordingly.

With a circular saw, create a saw kerf down the middle of the bottom of the bar; it needn't extend all the way to the ends, but doing so will make it simpler to cut the top bars. The groove must be the width of your saw blade and at least 1/8" deep. Make this groove, then fill it with melted beeswax and let it cool. When the frames are in place, your bees will have a foundation on which to construct their beeswax.

ASSEMBLING THE HIVE

You must first assemble your materials, and cut and glue all of the boards to the specifications specified above. Create the sides and ends first, then construct the crucial follower boards while the glue is setting.

To accomplish this, place a 17" top bar along the top edge of each of your follower boards using glue, screws, or pins. To help guarantee that the wood is laterally oriented while doing this, insert thin strips of wood underneath. While they are setting, clamp the wood pieces together.

An 11" or 12" board that is 1/2" thick is required to create the follower boards. Mark the board with a 15" marker at the top and a 7 1/2" marker halfway down.

Draw a line from top to bottom through each mark, then make 2 1/2"-wide marks on either side of the point at the bottom edge.

To create a trapezoidal shape, connect the bottom and top dots—not the central line. To save wood, extend your shape to create an identical upside-down shape on the opposite side.

Along the top edge of each follower board, glue, pin, or screw a top bar (centered). Place a clamp on them and let them dry overnight.

MAKING THE LEGS

You'll require four legs, each measuring 3" at a height that you prefer, by 2" (75 x 50mm) (typically around 30"). A wheelchair user's must be at least 26" tall, which may be more fitting.

If you don't want to use legs, this hive will function just as well sitting on a stand or base; just make sure it's stable. The only thing that matters is that your hive is not directly on the ground, as this will make it a haven for many pests.

If employing legs, they must be fastened to your hive's end pieces using 2" bolts and stainless steel or galvanized nuts. Put washers under the bolt and nut heads to stop them from scratching the wood.

AVOID USING WOOD SCREWS. Yes, they are far less expensive, but they are also unreliable and almost always result in tragedy.

The first thing to do is to reverse your follower boards. You should space them between 18" and 24" apart on your bench, parallel to one another.

To make the side of the hive, place one of your side panels flush against the follower boards and resting on the top bars.

Place the opposite side panel there.

When both of your side panels are in place, attach an end piece to one of the ends, with its bottom edge flat on the bench. For the top bars, this provides clearance space.

Draw a line with a pencil where the borders of the side panel touch the end piece after placing the end piece in place (inside and outside of the side panel).

Remove the end pieces, then mark three spots inside the

shape (where the side panels will ultimately sit) where you will drill screw holes. No matter how evenly spaced the screws are, it doesn't matter how precisely they are placed; just try to eyeball it (and not too close to the ends).

Use a drill bit for the hole that is slightly larger than the screw shank. Stainless steel or brass screws at least 2 1/2" long are what you need to use for this component.

To save time, stack the two end pieces on top of one another with the guide-topped one on top. Then, drill pilot holes where you had previously designated. To ensure that the boards don't slide when you're screwing them, place some screws in the holes after you drill the first few.

If you're utilizing legs, use the time you have to drill to make some bolt holes in your legs. Mark a position 5" from the top of your leg (in the middle) and then draw a straight line down to the bottom of your leg. The outside of your leg will lie along this line. Drill a lower hole 10" from the top and a hole no less than 3" from the edge of the leg. You will have the top of your leg cut to make room for the lid. Be sure the lower hole is comfortably positioned outside the sidewall line. If you're uncertain, use the holes in your end pieces as a guide to determine where to drill the holes in the legs.

As previously stated, the legs will support the roof frame. Mark a straight line down the top edge of your end piece, which should be about 2" from the top of your leg, as you align your legs with your end pieces. Make an indentation with a saw, but stop short of cutting all the way through.

FOR THE FLOOR (MESH)

As we've previously explained, it's preferable to utilize a solid floor during colder months, but mesh flooring is much better for most of the year and for simple hive maintenance.

For the task, we advise utilizing heavy-duty plastic garden mesh because it is both durable and adaptable.

Simply place your mesh on the floor of the cavity of the hive and cut it to fit the opening as precisely as possible.

It's an excellent idea to cut some rough pieces of wood and use them within the mesh as a kind of doorstop to make sure it's sealed tightly and nothing can get in. Make sure to cut these pieces precisely to match the contours of your follower boards.

A 6" x 3/4" piece of wood can be placed under your hive and secured with metal snap locks, hinges, etc. if you wish to utilize a solid floor.

ENTRANCE

Your bees need a way in now that you have some sort of box for them to live in. To do this, drill a few holes—at least three are advised—at least 1" in diameter and 2" away from the base of your hive. The entrances should be placed close to one another in the middle of the side of the hive but leave at least 3" between each hole.

A few more entrances can be added on the opposite side, or you can add another one at least 4" or 5" from the end of the hive.

ROOF FRAME

Finally, use the aforementioned screws to attach your legs before assembling the frame.

The roof structure is a straightforward rectangle made of 3" x 3/4" wood with screws or glue fastened to the corners. Remember to leave about 1/4" slack in both directions to accommodate wood movement; if your roof clogs, it will be quite inconvenient.

ROOF

Plastic corrugated sheets work well for making modest roofs. In the winter, it's not the best option for isolation, but it works as a quick fix.

To make a decision that looks more exquisite, choose a triangular gable roof. This is particularly preferable during rainy seasons because the water will just roll off. You can use any material, but it's best to go with something lightweight.

FINISHING TOUCHES

To shield your hive from the weather, coat it as a last step.

The majority of beekeepers advise using Cuprinol, paint, Creosote, or varnishes to coat your hive, though you may omit this step if you utilized red cedar wood in its place.

The linseed and beeswax remedy, which we previously stated, will be described here along with a recipe.

Heat in a double boiler (or a bain Marie) a mixture of 1:20 linseed oil to melt beeswax (like 1-liter raw linseed oil to 50ml beeswax).

Stir for 10 minutes while heating as hot as you can.

While still somewhat heated, paint onto your hive and allow to cool a little.

When painting, be sure to coat the underside of nail heads, joints, and end grain.

The bees will coat the interior of the hive, so you don't need to coat.

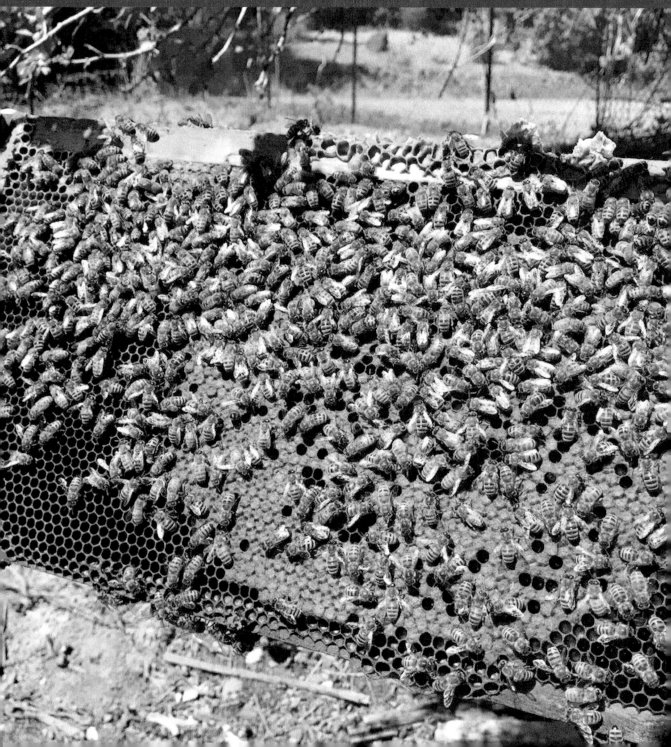

The first year of beekeeping will be a learning experience for you. For you and your bees, this year is one of firsts. You might get your first sting, but you might also get your first taste of local honey. Consider this chapter to be a season-by-season checklist of all the things that need to be accomplished. You'll be an expert at beekeeping after your first year and know what to do in each season, from winter feeding through spring honey flow.

Most apiarists place their bee orders for spring delivery. However, you might be able to purchase them throughout the year depending on the environment where you live. This seasonal almanac will be accurate no matter the time of year or when you bring your bees indoors. I'm going to describe this beekeeping year as though you got your bees in the spring to save paper and time. If you need to, you can make

adjustments as needed.

The First Two Months

Consider that the flowers are just beginning to bloom and that you have just put in your new bees. Keep the feeder filled with the bee food recipe from this page and make sure your bees have access to fresh water each day.

In order to monitor your bees' behavior throughout the first two months, you must check on them every day. In this passage, I'm referring to the observations I made outside the hive. To ensure the queen has been freed, if you purchased a pack of bees, you should undertake your initial check three to five days after installing your bees in addition to daily monitoring. Following your observation that the colony has welcomed its new queen, you will check every other week for roughly a month. The bees should be left alone to do their thing during the spring nectar flow after your first couple of hive checks.

Spring, the First Year

It is crucial for beekeepers to become knowledgeable about the nearby nectar flows. For further information, get in touch with your neighborhood garden club, beekeepers group, or county extension office. When there isn't enough nectar, you should feed your bees; when there is, you should hold back so they can forage for food. This depends on the nectar flow.

This spring, your bees are new to the region. They will take numerous orientation flights to become acquainted with the area's forage and water resources. This is why having plants in your yard for pollinators is a smart idea.

NO HONEY FOR YOU

I hope you have patience if you entered beekeeping solely for the liquid treasure known as honey. It's likely that you won't gather your first crop of honey until the following spring. For their survival this year, your bees will need time to construct comb, establish their colony, and store honey. If there is a good nectar flow this spring and summer, there may be a fall harvest. But realistically, wait at least a year before planning to collect honey. It's worth the wait, I promise.

Spring, the Second Year

The time of year when bees are busiest is spring. You'll see that the bees have yellow legs as they return to the hive after emerging from their winter hibernation. Those are pollen baskets on their back legs, which are carrying pollen. The workers are busy raising brood inside the hive, while the queen is occupied with egg production. When the nectar flow begins and you notice the bees collecting pollen, you can stop feeding them. Regardless of nectar flow or season, you should always provide fresh water.

APRIL SHOWERS BRING PROBLEMS

Although rain may be beneficial for your gardens and plants, it is not beneficial for bees. In the rain, bees will not forage. Because the bees will be starving and have a lot of brood to feed, it is crucial to pay close attention to the rains in the spring. In addition to the fact that rain prevents bees from foraging, it also washes pollen away and dilutes honey. In other words, even after the rain has stopped, it takes some time for the plants to recuperate enough to give the bees all they require.

Regardless of the time of year, if you're having a very wet season, you should give your bees some bee food to keep them from going hungry.

Summer

The bees forage continuously all morning, all day, and even all night long throughout the summer. The bees can gather more pollen, nectar, and water since the days are longer. During the summer, when everyone is busy getting ready for the next winter, your colony will be at its most populous.

If you haven't already, take off your entrance reducer right now. If you don't, your hive risks overheating. In order to stay cool throughout the summer, the bees will beard on the outside of the hive, which will result in less activity.

Fall

The bees' final chance to gather their crop before the long winter is in the fall. This is the season's final nectar and honey flow. Bees take advantage of the summer plants going to seed, so they may produce more honey to preserve for the chilly winter.

Fall is another season when you should be mindful of the blooming flowers, the rainy days, and the activity of your bees. Are they still making their way back to the hive on yellow legs? Bees will consume their winter stores if they don't have enough to forage on during the fall. Therefore, if they are not fed now, they will starve in the upcoming months. For them to preserve their honey for the winter, it is best to feed them now.

Winter

For the beekeeper, winter is a rather dull season. There is not much going on outside for you to see because everything is happening inside the beehive. Maintaining the queen bee's health and wellbeing is your bees' primary task over the winter. Everything else stops producing. Now, it's all about the queen and the strongest individuals surviving.

In order to stay warm, bees spend the winter inside their hive. Your bees will begin to cluster in the center of their hive as soon as the temperature falls into the low 50s. With changes in temperature, this cluster will grow and shrink. When the temperature is higher, it will expand; when the temperature is lower, it will contract.

The older bees will be on the cluster's periphery, with the queen at its core. The bees rotate their cluster around the hive while they eat their honey. To survive the winter, the bees depend on their honey reserves. Many bees are on the verge of starvation by the time spring arrives and the nectar begins to flow because they have consumed all of their honey supplies.

Lifting the back of the hive is one method for winter bee monitoring without opening the hive. What's the weight? You must feed them if it is light; a lack of weight indicates a lack of honey. Put your ear as close to the hive as possible to check on them during the winter. A hive in motion sounds like a tiny engine running. A sound emanating from your hive should be heard, thus it may be alarming if you don't.

Chapter 11
All About Honey

The entire process of honey production and harvesting is covered in this chapter. Such a tasty reward! Remember, beekeeping is a journey; something this luxurious takes time to make. It shouldn't be considered competition or a quick-fix pastime. In my opinion, honey is a bee's way of expressing "thank you" for protecting it for a year and giving it food and water when it was in need. A bee will express its appreciation for you by giving you honey, a lovely golden present.

First Things: What is Honey?

Honey is essentially cured and treated with nectar. When pollen and nectar are scarce, bees mainly rely on honey as their only food supply. Some individuals could call honey "bee vomit." Are they in the right? Okay, somewhat, but not quite. Bees have a honey sac, which is a pouch located at the base of their throat. Bees transform nectar in the honey sac by adding enzymes and digesting the nectar to produce honey. In their honey sac, they keep the nectar until they return to the hive.

How Bees Make Honey

Numerous worker bees leave the hive to search for pollen and nectar. Nectar from plants and flowers is consumed by them, and they store it in their honey sac where it combines with enzymes. They then take off for the hive where they deliver their nectar to a different worker bee known as a house bee. The house bee then performs the same procedure again, but this time, she transports the nectar to the comb cells, where it turns into honey.

Just as you would reduce a liquid in cooking to make

it thicker, the bees fan the honey to aid in the liquid's evaporation. The honey is still green at this time, meaning the bees haven't finished processing it enough for human use, and it could soon deteriorate. Once the liquid has been sufficiently reduced, it is capped (beeswax is used to seal it) for long-term storage. It is honey once the cap is on.

It Takes a Lot of Bees

Bees give a whole new meaning to the phrase "being worked to death." I understand that some of you may feel as though you work nonstop, but bees truly do that. They start working toward the greater good of their hives from the time they crawl out of their cage. Just thirty more days of nonstop work on this planet, no poolside honeycombs, no beehive retirement village.

Foraging bees will go up to 5 miles from their home in search of plants. The majority of people would go hungry if they had to trek as far to obtain food as bees do. Keep this in mind when considering potential exposures for your bees. Your bees will still browse at the closest chemical facility even if

you have the nicest organic garden around. Because of this, finding fully organic honey is hard. There may be hazardous compounds present in some of the plants the bees visit.

During its lifetime, a bee only makes around 1/12 of a teaspoon of honey. One pound of honey will need the aggregate flight of 55,000 bees, or roughly 55,000 miles, from an average beehive. Take a moment to process that.

For every pound of honey you purchase at the grocery store, approximately 770 bees traveled roughly 55,000 miles to produce it. This implies that they had to make numerous flower visits in order to fill the plastic bear you just purchased—in excess of 2 million. Just for a single pound of honey. Do you comprehend why we refer to this substance as liquid gold?

You should think about how crucial plants are to both human survival and the survival of bees as you read this and consider its significance. Bees require bees, bees require plants, and we require plants. Life has a circle to it. Beekeepers and gardeners are inseparable, in my opinion; neither can live alone. The fruits, vegetables, and flowers you plant can also be harvested as an added bonus. The situation benefits both parties.

How Much Honey will One Hive Produce?

The annual honey production of an active beehive might exceed 200 pounds. Since Langstroth's hives are the most prevalent, let's focus on them for the purposes of this discussion. The weight of the deep box, when loaded with honey, may be around 70 pounds, the middlebox about 50 pounds, and the short box about 40 pounds.

You will increase the number of boxes in your hive as your colony expands and honey output increases. In certain situations, your hive may contain five or six boxes, all of which contain honey or brood. One person may be unable to manage the enormous weight of a fully loaded hive. Because of this, I implore you to get assistance. On the day of harvest, a beekeeper can always use some free honey as an incentive to assist in lifting big beehives.

These numbers are merely an illustration, of course. Your actual honey output will depend on a number of factors including the amount of rain, the forage that is available, and the colony's overall health. When you are daydreaming about all the liquid gold you will be swimming in while salivating over honey, remember how much honey the bees will need to conserve for themselves in order to survive the winter.

In this chapter, the fundamentals of beeswax, one of the primary materials you can obtain from your beehive, will be covered. We'll go over the production process, collection methods, and applications for beeswax in a concise manner.

What Exactly is It?

Beeswax is a type of organic wax that is used by worker bees to create "combs" that will eventually hold their honey. Additionally, it is frequently used to recycle and repair preexisting combs.

The primary components of beeswax are fatty acids and natural alcohol. The wax is produced by a particular gland in the abdomen of worker bees, which essentially converts pollen's sugar into the wax by processing it; the pollen they gather contributes to the wax's "golden" hue.

In addition to being ideal for building the hive, beeswax is a terrific ingredient for cosmetic products like lip balm because it is so durable and stable (particularly in hot and cold weather conditions).

Fun fact: Bees must ingest five to six days' worth of pollen to generate beeswax.

Benefits of Beeswax

Beeswax is used as a common ingredient in a wide variety of products, from food to cosmetics, for many good reasons. Here are a few of the most intriguing ones:

Due to the fact that it is insoluble in water, it is incredibly practical as a sealant for wood protection or for use in crafts. This is also the rationale for our recommendation to combine it with linseed oil before using it to seal your wooden beehive.

Making candles with beeswax is one of the best uses for the material because the wax burns cleanly and doesn't emit smoke or chemicals. According to some, burning beeswax releases negative ions that purify the air by removing "positive charge" airborne contaminants like dust.

Beeswax has a relatively low melting point of 63 degrees Celsius (about 145 degrees Fahrenheit), which makes it quite simple to transform it from a solid to a liquid for use in a variety of applications.

Beeswax is far from a straightforward substance; it contains more than 250 different elements such as acids, long-chain alkanes, esters, and others. Hentriacontane makes up around 9% of beeswax, which is why it is so stable and insoluble in water.

How Can I Use Beeswax?

You've come to the correct place if you have beeswax on hand and are unsure of what to do with it. There are many more applications for beeswax than those we have listed below.

Never throw away beeswax since it is so helpful and versatile.

- Cosmetics ingredients (lip balm etc.)
- Pharmaceutical uses
- Official documents seal
- Skincare ingredients (soap etc.)
- Woodcare
- Food production
- Crafts
- Waxing products
- Candles

You may find out more about its usage in detail by conducting additional studies.

How to Harvest Beeswax

We'll go over the best way to accomplish it below if you want to extract beeswax yourself. The "Melt and Strain Method" is what is used in this process.

1. Collect the "Capping" and Comb

Remove the caps off your frames with a tool (just the wax that covers the combs). While you should make every effort to get all of the honey out, some may inevitably come out. Don't stress about it too much; we'll strain the honey later.

After gathering the comb, place it in cheesecloth to drain the honey (place the fabric over a container to capture the honey to prevent a mess!).

2. Separate the Wax From the "Debris."

Place the cheesecloth-wrapped beeswax bundle inside a small bundle and into a pan of simmering water. If there are any large lumps, you can press them down with anything like a wooden spoon or stick to assist the wax to melt more quickly.

Boiling water should be used, and after the beeswax has completely melted, it should be squeezed to extract as much liquid as possible. The cheesecloth should then be removed from the pot, leaving "wax water" behind.

The solution should be poured into a container and left to cool. All of the filthy water will eventually sink below the wax, which will eventually rise to the surface. We must clean the wax "cake" above because it will still be unclean.

3. Clean the Wax Cake

After the solid wax cake has completely cooled, remove it from the liquid and remelt it. When it becomes liquid again, any leftover bad stuff is removed by passing it through a filter while it is still hot.

4. Put into a Mold

You ought to now have some beautiful, clean wax. If necessary, use it as a liquid or pour it into any mold you have, and you're done!

Don't overlook one of the most valuable and plentiful components of your hive, beeswax, as there are so many fantastic uses for it.

I know you were all enthusiastic about the liquid gold and perhaps even the possibility of making money from keeping one or two hives. However, protecting the species is beekeeping's top concern and primary focus. Learning about the diseases and pests that can harm them is necessary. Bees, unlike some other animals, typically let you know when something is wrong. If your bees have any health issues, I will explain what to check for and offer possible solutions during hive inspections.

The key to keeping your hive healthy is to observe it regularly and record everything in your beekeeping journal. You can spot any changes in your bees by keeping a daily eye on them. Then, by occasionally going over your beekeeping record, you may compare seasons from one year to the next or, if you have multiple hives, even compare hives.

Why Do Bees Get Sick?

The species of honeybees has endured for countless millennia. Despite their seeming fragility, they are actually incredibly durable. Despite our best efforts, honeybees are wild insects that are tenaciously motivated to survive. No one has ever succeeded in keeping bees alive without giving them access to nature.

However, over time, it appears that more exposure to poisons and chemicals had an impact on their immune system. Beekeepers are searching for alternate treatment options because the disease treatments they have been using for the past 30 years are no longer as effective.

While many of the causes of bee illnesses are wholly beyond human control, some can be avoided. Your bees could become ill for a variety of reasons, including:

- Being cooped up inside for an extended period of time
- Climate
- Exposure to hazardous substances
- Bacteria and virus exposure
- Overcrowding
- Too much moisture
- Insects and arachnids in the hive

- Starvation
- Too much room

Preventing Illness

As I previously stated, some aspects of your surroundings are wholly beyond our control; one example of this is the time I lost two entire colonies as a result of our county's use of chemical sprays to try to reduce mosquitoes in the neighborhood. On occasion, nevertheless, we can contribute to the prevention of stress and illness. Even though some of these things won't kill your bees on their own, others can impair their immune systems, making them more prone to disease and pests.

By expanding your hive with more boxes or supers or by dividing your colony to provide room for expansion, you can avoid overcrowding.

A concern with having too much space is that it allows for the growth of pests and predators. A hive that is too large for bees to defend and protect is difficult for them to do. Imagine a huge Hollywood gala with numerous entryways and a single bouncer at the door. There is no way that one bouncer could keep all the riffraff out. The same logic holds true when there are too many bees and not enough bees in the hive. This occurs when novice beekeepers try to fill their hive with all the boxes at once.

When a hive separates from a swarm or, occasionally, after the winter when a sizable section of the colony dies, a hive may also have too much space. To avoid this, make sure to get rid of any unused boxes and wait to add a new box until the bees have completed building comb on 34 of the existing frames.

It's simple to stop the bees from starving. Water and honey, or bee nourishment, are essential for your bees to survive.

Your bees might be starving even when you assume there is plenty of food available for them to forage. When conducting inspections, keep fresh water on hand at all times and make sure their food supply or honey reserves are stocked. Create some food storage so they can survive the winter as well.

Numerous factors, such as illness, a shortage of food, predators, a new habitat, and excessive human meddling, can stress bees. But a major cause of bee stress is a lack of food and the excessive foraging that results from that. For this reason, I suggest that you plant your bee garden before erecting your hives.

SIGNS OF SICKNESS

The value of observation and keeping a beekeeping notebook cannot be overstated. Even anything as straightforward as "Bees are flying a lot today" might be noted. Trust me, you'll be glad you took thorough notes.

Observable signs that anything is wrong that you can see from outside the hive include:

Excessive amounts of dead bees: There are various interpretations for this. You can rule out potential causes by reading about all of the diseases and pests in this chapter. Starvation, the bees freezing to death, an abundance of wetness, or chemical exposure are possible additional explanations.

Lack of activity: When there isn't much activity and it's not winter, it's time to open your hive and look inside.

Outside the hive, there might be a lot more bee poop than normal.

Things you can see inside the hive that may be a sign that something isn't quite right include:

Missing queen: Also get in touch with your bee mentor and a nearby or online beekeeper who offers queens. Without the queen, a colony cannot thrive.

More than one egg per cell: If there are too many eggs in each cell, you have egg-laying workers. Because worker eggs are not fertilized, they will all develop into drones. Additionally, a colony doesn't require that many drones because they will consume all the resources without contributing to any effort.

Foul smell: The foul smell is not the same as the nasty stench emanating from a sickly brood. You may have AFB if you smell something bad.

Funny-looking brood: It refers to something that appears unusual.

The hive is not being cleaned by the bees.

The bees are generating numerous queen cells, supersedure cells, or queen cells out of regular brood cells.

The Most Common Pests and What to Do About Them

Beehives may become infested by pathogenic bacteria, fungi, viruses, mites, and pests. In spite of all the chaos that bees may encounter, a healthy hive can perform an amazing job of defending its colony. Cleaners in hives are always working to keep the hive and all the bees clean. For further security at their home's entrance, they keep guard bees.

But there will be occasions when you have to intervene and assist them. If you find yourself having to treat your hive, be careful to alternate your treatments to prevent the bacteria and pests from developing a tolerance to whatever you are doing.

American Foulbrood (AFB) and European Foulbrood EFB)

The spore-forming bacteria that cause AFB and EFB are infectious and extremely contagious diseases. The larvae and pupae are affected, not the adult bees. The hive gets a bad stench from this sickness, hence the name.

The evidence is visible in the brood cells in addition to the smell. Infected larvae change color to a caramel-chocolate shade and dissolve into a gooey mess on the cell floor as

opposed to normal pearly-white larvae. After the cell is sealed, they always perish. AFB is more serious than EFB (although still very dangerous). The larvae of an EFB infection are twisted inside the brood cell and start out as an off-white color before turning brown. They pass away before the cell is sealed.

Also Check For:
- A spotted pattern on the brood
- Off-center holes in the brood cell caps
- Sunken cappings on the brood cells
- Caramel color of dead larvae
- Scales on the larvae

You must get in touch with your neighborhood extension office or beekeepers association if you think you may have AFB or EFB. State legislation may govern how infected hives are handled and disposed of. Unfortunately, there is no salvaging your colony if it contracts AFB or EFB. Once you've been in touch with your county extension, they will either come to dispose of your hive for you or they will provide you instructions. Extreme precautions must be used because the spores can live permanently on beekeeping equipment and are highly contagious.

VARROA MITE

The parasitic Varroa mite feeds on honeybee blood and the blood of the young. Only a honeybee colony is capable of reproducing it. The bees become less strong and live less time due to these vampire arachnids. The mature female mite has eight legs and a flattened oval-shaped body that is reddish brown in color. These annoyances should be visible to the unaided eye.

You can use a variety of chemical remedies to get rid of Varroa mites. They consist of oxalic acid, Apistan, CheckMite+, Apistan, Mite Away Quick Strips, Formic Pro, Apivar, Hopguard II, Apivar Life Var, and Apistan. There will be specific application instructions for each therapy.

DEFORMED WING VIRUS

Although it can occur in colonies that haven't been infected with Varroa, this viral disease is linked to infestations with those mites. It could result in bees developing wings that are deformed, twisted, or wrinkled. These bees are obviously unable to fly and are unable to assist their colony. Controlling the Varroa mite population is the best strategy for combating the deformed-wing virus.

SACBROOD

A virus called sacbrood attacks a honeybee brood, primarily worker bee larvae. With inconsistent cappings present throughout the brood cells, the sacbrood virus generates an uneven brood pattern. Because it inhibits the brood from reaching the pupa stage, this disease is relatively simple to identify.

In most situations, a strong hive can defeat sacbrood disease on its own, while severe cases can necessitate replacing the queen.

BEE LOUSE

An infrequent pest of bees, the bee louse is a tiny, wingless member of the fly family. Although it is not a sickness of the bees, it does cause a lot of stress on colonies, which makes them weaker.

Although they only have six legs, bee-louse adults resemble Varroa mites somewhat. Adults should add a small amount of tobacco to their smoker and puff on the hive to treat their condition. Despite having a worm-like appearance, the larvae are very difficult to discern with the unaided eye. Than real larvae, comb damage is more likely to be observed. The frames should be wrapped in plastic and frozen for 48 hours to kill any bee-louse larvae present. By doing so, you'll guarantee that both adults and larvae are killed.

TRACHEAL MITE

This small spider is a respiratory system parasite that attacks honeybees. Drones, queen bees, and worker bees are all susceptible to infection. The bee is killed after it consumes

blood and reproduces inside its breathing tubes. Indicators include an increase in winter fatalities and a decrease in spring brood production.

If you think you may have tracheal mites, your county extension office could arrange a test. The recommended course of action includes requeening the hive along with the use of menthol and fat patties consisting of vegetable shortening and sugar (which prevent mite reproduction).

WAX MOTH

Beeswax combs, comb honey, and pollen harvested by bees are all harmed by the bug known as the wax moth. For weak colonies, they are primarily a problem. Even if you're the best beekeeper in the world, wax moths are a problem that all hives must deal with eventually.

Reduce the amount of empty space in your hive to help fend off a wax moth invasion. Add boxes only if your hive actually requires them. Wax moths will take control of the hive if no one is present to protect it. Wrapping the affected frame in a plastic bag and freezing it for 48 hours is another method of treating wax moth infestations. Additionally, you can fumigate your colony using crystals of paradichlorobenzene (PDB).

SMALL HIVE BEETLE

Nearly all honeybee hives are home to this invasive insect. Small hive beetles will proliferate if given the chance and seriously harm your colony. Nearly all beekeepers will have to deal with them, just like the wax moth.

Although there are various pharmaceutical remedies, little hive beetle avoidance is the greatest line of protection. Limit the amount of space that is available in the hive, just like with the wax moth. Apply a board with a wire bottom and a tray underneath it to the bottom of your Warre or Langstroth hive. On the tray, spread some dish soap. The insects will drop into the tray and become trapped there.

Critters to Watch Out For

Do you ever wonder how bees have survived all these years? They excel at surviving, in my opinion. If there were this many creatures following me, I would dig myself a hole and never emerge. Critters of all shapes and sizes are driven insane and transformed into hive raiders by that liquid gold, which no other bug or animal can produce. There are several things you can do to safeguard your bees, albeit you cannot ensure their safety.

Ants: Cinnamon should be scattered all around the beehive's base. Although you have to repeat it frequently, this strategy is one that I have done, and it works beautifully. To ensure

we have sufficient on hand, we get several sizable containers of cinnamon from a cheap store.

Other bees: Details are included in Robber Bees below.

Spiders: It's rumored that spiders dislike mint. To keep spiders and other insects away from your hive, put some nearby. Make sure to clear any webs from your beehives' exterior or surroundings.

Mice: If you're experiencing trouble with mice entering your hive, you can utilize the entrance reducer if the weather is not too hot. Mice will consume the bees' comb but won't harm the bees.

Frogs: Consider relocating a frog's habitat, which includes moist spots, rocks, and anything they can hide under, further away from your beehives. In all honesty, frogs won't consume enough bees to harm the colony until, of course, they devour the queen.

Birds: Bees in flight will be eaten by birds, but they won't bother your hive. They typically won't eat enough to endanger your colony, just like the frogs.

Other mammals: You can fasten flooring tack strips, such as those used to hold the carpet down, to plywood to deter raccoons, badgers, weasels, foxes, skunks, and perhaps bears. These strips should be laid out in front of the hive so that anyone approaching it will tread on the tacks.

Robber Bees

Bees will steal honey from other bees, which may come as a bit of a shock to you. They desire what their neighbor has, even among insects. The existence of their own colony is all that matters to bees, notwithstanding their intense devotion to preserving the colony's survival. When the nectar flow is low, such as in the fall or other seasons, a stronger bee colony will steal the honey from a weaker colony.

It could be challenging for a beginner beekeeper to determine whether another hive is robbing your hive. Indicators of this theft do exist, though. For instance, if you notice two bees huddled together or two bees battling at the front of the hive, this is a sign of robbers. Another sign is the presence of dead bees with stingers by the entrance to the hive in the autumn. (Fall-season dead bees without stingers by the hive's entrance are the drones being expelled before winter.) This is also a sign of thieves if you detected chew marks on the comb of the honey jars and a punctured or missing top.

Install an entrance reducer if it's not too hot, or a thin mesh wire across the front if it is, to deter robbers from entering your hive. Security bees will have less room to guard as a result of this.

As you progress through your first season of beekeeping, you'll change from a novice to an expert. Every season will teach you something new; even beekeepers with 20 years of expertise are always picking up new skills. I've never seen a beekeeper who said they became bored or tired of what they did, which is the beautiful thing about beekeeping.

Without a doubt, it's not always simple. I wanted to give up after chemical drift cost us two colonies. We emptied our hives and stored them behind the shed so that we would never use them again. Nature, however, had different ideas; she wanted us to maintain bees. Months after we placed our hives in storage, we heard a faint buzzing sound as we walked behind the shed. And there they were—feral bees living in our hives! Honeybees are magnificent, strong, and free. Once more, my heart felt full. Furthermore, the strongest and most durable colonies are frequently formed by swarms of feral bees.

Do You Need More Than One Hive?

How many hives you should have is something I didn't mention previously. Please note that backyard beekeepers are the target audience for this book; commercial beekeepers were not the intended audience. I'm going to strongly advise you to get two or more hives. Why are there two? Everything, including beehives, works better in pairs.

Compare and contrast: Having a benchmark to compare to will be helpful if you're a beginning beekeeper. If you notice something odd about one of your hives, you can compare it to the others to see whether it is "normal."

You will have a backup: You will have a backup hive in case you lose a queen or a hive for whatever reason. I've previously lost one hive, then the remaining hive split with a swarm in the spring, giving me two hives once more. If you lose one and it was your only hive, you will have to start over.

Combine efforts: You will need to requeen your hive if it is the only one and it is weak. There's still a risk it won't make it through that. To create a stronger hive, you can combine two hives if one of them is weaker.

Save money: No, it doesn't cost twice as much to have twice as many hives, despite what you would think. One honey extractor, one hive tool, and one bee suit, for instance, are still all that are required. The costs can be split between the two colonies in many cases.

Double the honey: If you intend to sell your extras, having two hives means you'll have twice as much liquid gold and, thus, twice as much money.

Don't Fear the Swarm

Beekeepers may welcome swarms or fear them as a warning. Those who want to grow their apiary are thrilled to observe swarm indicators since it indicates they can acquire a free additional bee colony. Recap: A swarm occurs when the old queen and half of your colony leave the hive in search of a new home. The new queen and the rest of your bees will begin work on establishing their colony. Swarming indicates that a colony is healthy and expanding, hence it is a positive indicator. You might be sorry to see them depart, though, if you don't want your colony to expand.

It is absolutely fantastic to observe a swarm. We could hear the buzzing of our bees from inside the house when they swarmed. Once you know what it sounds like, their acoustic roar is easily distinguished.

The first queen and roughly half of the workers will be in the swarm. In a different manner than bearding, they will begin to gather together and hang around on the hive's exterior. They will stay in a group in a high location once they have left the hive until the scouts locate them a new home. The bees are extremely submissive and devoted to guarding the queen during a swarm; they are not interested in you at all. When bees are swarming, your chance of being stung is the lowest.

An indication of swarming, in addition to the obvious outward indications, is an increase in queen cells within the hive. Giving your bees more space will prevent them from swarming, which is something you should do if you don't want them to. Your hive needs more frames to accommodate its growth.

Contact your local association or beekeeping mentor if you notice swarming indicators. They can assist you in capturing the swarm for your own use or in giving it to another beekeeper. It's a fantastic strategy to increase the population of bees and honey.

A Royal Coup

The colony's queen is the most significant bee. The colony would not succeed without her. The colony's survival, development, and health are all determined by the queen. Each and every bee has a necessary and significant duty, but none is more significant than the queen. Because the queen is so crucial, you might occasionally need to remove her from power and/or install a new queen in her place. Beekeepers refer to this procedure as "requeening."

Queenless: You've looked inside your hive and discovered the absence of a queen. She might not be there, or you could notice other indications that the hive is queenless. A queenless hive can be identified by many eggs in one cell, which indicates that worker bees are currently laying eggs. Another indication of a queenless hive is the formation of several queen cells.

Squished the queen: Although regrettable, it does occur. Perhaps it happened while you were replacing the frames, harvesting honey, or inspecting the hive. Accidents do occur, and in certain cases, you urgently need a new queen.

Aging queen: Queen bees have a three to four-year lifespan, although their first and second years are when they are most productive. If your queen hasn't been replaced by the hive on its own by the end of her second year, I advise doing so in order to maintain a healthy and productive hive.

Rejection: Even while it happens infrequently, the colony occasionally rejects the queen outright.

Sick queen: The worker bees provide food for the queen. In some instances, the workers can infect the queen with illness or disease.

Lack of pheromones: The pheromones of a queen cause the hive's workers to respond. The hive will behave erratically if the queen is unable to create enough pheromones.

Requeening

It's crucial to have the new queen ready before getting rid of the old one if your current queen is still in the hive and you need to replace her for any reason. To find out if anyone is raising queens for sale, you can either acquire a queen from a provider or get in touch with a beekeeper's group. My own experience indicates that new queens typically cost $30 or more.

When you think about it, everyone in the colony is related to the queen. Every bee carries her DNA in its veins. They know each other personally. In the event that the queen must be changed for any reason, the hive must go through the acceptance procedure once more, exactly as if you were putting in a new colony of bees with a caged queen.

You must get rid of the old queen after installing the new one in your hive. Leave her head alone! Although it may sound harsh, there are instances when it's important for the colony's well-being and survival.

Let's have a look at some general tips and guidance for beehive care and maintenance. Taking care of your colony and keeping your hive healthy go hand in hand. Bees that live in a healthy hive are content.

First off, while the quantity of upkeep required for your hive can change, it's crucial to maintain some consistency during this period. You will get more out of it if you put more effort into it, just like with any abilities and interests.

Your bees will create considerably higher-quality materials if you keep up with beekeeping properly. Additionally, your bees will be much healthier, happier, and more productive (and they won't be as prone to swarm).

The majority of specialists concur that the best honey harvest occurs in the spring when beehives need the most upkeep.

Steps To Maintain your Hive

A beekeeper must follow a number of steps to maintain their hive:

1. GENERAL REPARATIONS

Your beehive will gradually lose strength and become less livable for your bees. The weather, which can result in problems like warping, rotting, cracking, and rusting, is the main cause of this. Larger animals and insects can potentially harm your hive.

Your hive needs to have any visibly damaged pieces repaired as soon as possible. If they can no longer be fixed, they must be replaced.

You can make sure that your hive can withstand the environment and other harmful circumstances by frequently replacing and repairing damaged pieces. Additionally, it will keep your hive looking good!

2. ENTRANCE BLOCKING

It is only really required to use entry barriers during the winter. Beekeepers restrict the number of hive entrances to trap heat inside and reduce the need for bees to heat the

hive. Additionally, it keeps the ventilation at an adequate level and prevents the entry of other undesirable objects.

Your entrance may be blocked by:

- Using an entrance reducer
- Putting up a mesh or other perforated material with holes large enough for your bees to pass through over the entrance.
- Putting pieces of wood in some of the numerous entrances to the hive

3. EXCLUDERS AND SUPERS

The queen excluder, a layer that separates the brood from the comb, stops the queen from laying eggs in inappropriate places. When their honeycomb or brood combs are full, bees actually fill the space in supers with honey.

Using a queen excluder makes it much simpler to maintain your hive, so it will continue to function well. If you don't already have one, install one.

Aside from keeping your hive functioning properly, adding more supers will provide your bees with the extra storage they require during their busiest season (spring to summer).

4. REPLACE LOST BEESWAX

Bees use beeswax to line the inside of the hive to strengthen and improve comfort, as well as to create combs to hold their honey. It is therefore undesirable if any of it is damaged or lost.

A beekeeper might easily break off beeswax by accident when prying open their hive or removing frames. It happens rather frequently, and beeswax will be lost when honey is obtained. To avoid doing this, use a hive tool, but make sure you also attempt, if at all possible, to repair any broken wax.

You can buy natural replacement beeswax from a store or utilize extra wax from another hive if you need to replace huge chunks of wax.

5. SUFFICIENT VENTILATION

The interior of the hive may suffer serious harm if it is over- or under-ventilated. If the hive is not properly ventilated, water or even ice may develop inside, endangering both the hive's structure and the bees. Inadequate ventilation can also lead to the hive overheating, which can damage the structure and be uncomfortable for the bees. You'll see your bees engaging in particular actions, including bearding (see image) or fanning, when they're overheating.

6. WINDBREAKS

Beehives can suffer great damage from strong winds. In addition to pushing damp or chilly air into the cavity of the hive, it has the potential to overturn the entire structure, wiping out most of your bees' laborious efforts.

Think about adding a windbreaker to protect your hive from powerful winds. There are options made by humans as well as by nature (trees, shrubs, etc.).

Make sure to find out where the wind usually comes from in your neighborhood.
7. Rain Protection/Shade

Your hive might have major weather-related issues. The hive can be severely harmed by rainwater or any other type of moisture, which can also kill your bees or substantially upset them. The same unfortunate consequence can be caused by excessive direct sunshine.

It's a good idea to use an outer cover or a slanted cover to shield your hive from the rain so that the rain will roll off of it. It would be ideal if it were made of plastic or metal.

You can either make something to create shade or locate your hive in an area that will minimize direct light exposure.

If you decide to use a rain cover, be careful to take it off sometimes because doing so can hinder the hive's ability to ventilate properly. If your hive does unavoidably get too much water in it, set it up on a slight incline so that it can drain.

8. WOODLICE AND TERMITE PROTECTION

Beekeepers live in constant fear of pests like termites and woodlice. These critters can readily feed on your hive and gradually kill it because the majority of us choose to build our beehives out of wood. Termites and woodlice can easily hide inside rotten or old wood, and they are most vicious during the drier months.

You can use baits, liquid pesticides, or soil treatments to reduce the number of these pests. Find out the best solutions from your local beekeepers, and before using them, make sure your bees won't be harmed.

Additionally, you can stop them by clearing the vegetation from around your apiary.

9. PREDATOR PROTECTION

Several creatures, such as bears, mice, skunks, raccoons, etc., are likely to pose problems for your hive. Let's examine each of these in greater depth and offer possible fixes.

Bears enjoy eating honeycomb and destroying hives. If bears are a problem where you live, you can keep them away by enclosing your hive in a sturdy fence or boundary.

Mice are notorious for constructing nests in beehives, which can lead to a variety of issues for both you and your bees. By placing a mouse guard close to the entrance to your hive, you can keep mice away.

In addition to digging holes in hives, mice, and skunks frequently do so as well, destroying the comb and basically rendering the hive inhospitable. Making sure your hive is on a stand that is appropriately raised is the greatest approach to deter skunks.

Your beehive may sustain significant damage from raccoons as well. You may stop this by adding some sort of weight or lock to your hive's lid or roof because they frequently enter beehives through the lid to get inside.

Keep Things Clean

The last piece of advice I'll provide you is maintaining cleanliness. You may be familiar with the proverb "Cleanliness is next to godliness." In a beehive, it is undoubtedly true. A healthy beehive places great importance on cleanliness. It is very significant. In actuality, the beekeeper can transmit a lot of the infections that harm beehives.

Nearly all of your beekeeping equipment needs to be cleaned frequently. With hot water and soap, you can clean the majority of the equipment. Baking soda, vinegar, and washing soda are some of my preferred natural cleaners. I

only use bleach when it's necessary.

Hive tools: Use vinegar or combine bleach with water in a spray bottle or bucket to clean your hive tools. Do not combine the two solutions. Your cleaning supplies can be sprayed, wiped, or soaked, then dried. Your bee brush is part of this.

Bee feeder: Take care to thoroughly rinse after washing in warm, soapy water. Each time you add new bee food, follow these steps. Clean your feeder with a bleach solution if your colony was ill.

Water dishes: Remember to thoroughly rinse after washing in warm, soapy water. At least once per week, carry this out. Apply a bleach solution to your feeder to clean it if your colony was unwell.

Bee suit, gloves, and veil: There should be a label on your bee suit and gloves with washing instructions. I always hand wash the veil in the sink using warm, soapy water, rinse it, and then hang it to dry.

Beehive and frames: You must wash your hive before removing a frame or box, changing a board, or harvesting honey, especially if a hive was lost to illness or disease. It is crucial to wash the hive before adding bees if you purchased a secondhand one or received one as a gift. A large bucket or tub should contain one cup of bleach for five gallons of warm water. To remove any debris, use a wire scrub brush. Everything should spend 15 minutes soaking in the bleach water. Repeat the soaking, remove, and scrub if necessary. After cleaning everything, you can either store it in a sealed plastic bag for protection or allow everything to completely dry before putting it back in the hive.

Honey extraction equipment: Use warm, soapy water or warm water that has been combined with washing soda to clean all of the honey extraction machinery. Make sure to completely remove the honey from your tools. Before put-

ting it back in storage, give it a good rinse and dry.

Smoker: Just like your fireplace chimney, keeping your smoker clean and clear of buildup is essential. Your smoker's inside walls should be scraped using a wire brush. Eliminate any stray materials. Spray the remaining interior surfaces of the smoker with vinegar, then sprinkle baking soda on top. Then do it again. Remember to avoid getting your smoker's pump wet. The best ones I've found for this are tiny wire brushes that are roughly toothbrush size. When you finish using your smoker, or as soon as you see any black accumulation inside, clean it.

Sanitary beekeeping techniques will help shield your hive from the transmission of illness and disease. Do not attempt to clean this yourself if you have AFB or EFB, though. Inquire with the county extension. They will instruct you on how to disinfect every piece of equipment you have and may even demand that you burn your hive or frames.

Conclusion

So, Are You Ready to Start Beekeeping?

Thus, the conclusion is at hand. You now have all the information you need to establish a successful beekeeping business since I have shared everything I have learned from my years of expertise. Sincere gratification for your efforts to protect the insects that are essential to our life. It's astounding to consider it in that light, but it's true. Both the bees and we need each other.

Everyone can make a difference, whether they wish to raise bees for fun or as a business. Everyone you encounter will be happy to hear that you are keeping bees, as you will quickly discover. Before your beehive is put up, the demands for honey will begin to pour in.

Keep in mind that you can learn from others. Rely on your neighborhood beekeepers for assistance and refer back to this guide to troubleshoot and assist you with any issues you may have. The only thing I'm unable to provide you is practical experience. But you'll make it.

WILFRED C. BEATTY